PYTHON PROGRAMMING

FOR QUANTUM COMPUTING
USING QISKIT AND CIRQ

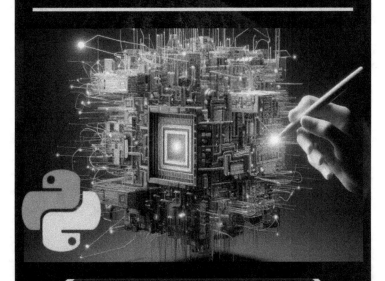

A Hands-on Guide to Quantum
Computing and Programming with
Python

RICHARD D. CROWLEY

Table of Contents

Mathematical Preliminaries for Quantum Computing Quantum computing, by its very nature, is deeply rooted in mathematics.1 To understand the behaviors of qubits, quantum gates, and quantum algorithms, a solid grasp of certain mathematical concepts is indispensable. Linear algebra, complex numbers, and Dirac notation form the bedrock upon which the entire edifice of quantum computation is built.

CHAPTER 3

Setting Up Your Quantum Programming
Environment   Before diving into the
exciting world of quantum algorithms
and applications, it's crucial to establish a
robust and efficient programming
environment. This involves installing the
necessary software, libraries, and tools
that will enable you to write, simulate,
and potentially run quantum programs

Quantum Error Correction and Fault Tolerance Quantum Error Correction (QEC) and Fault Tolerance are indispensable for the realization of practical quantum computers.1 Unlike classical computers, which are relatively robust to noise, quantum computers are extremely sensitive to environmental disturbances. This makes errors inevitable, necessitating sophisticated techniques to detect and correct them.

Part I:

Foundations of Quantum Computing

CHAPTER 1

Introduction to Quantum Computing

The 21st century is witnessing a technological revolution, and at its forefront lies quantum computing. While classical computers have served us remarkably well, pushing the boundaries of computation with each passing decade, they are fundamentally limited by the laws of classical physics. Certain problems, especially those involving complex simulations and vast datasets, remain intractable for even the most powerful supercomputers.[1] This is where quantum computing steps in, offering a radically different approach to information processing, one that leverages the bizarre yet powerful principles of quantum mechanics.

1.1 The Need for Quantum Computing.

The demand for quantum computing arises from the inherent limitations of classical computers in tackling specific classes of problems. Here are some key areas where classical computing falls short:

- **Complex Simulations:**
  - Simulating quantum systems, such as molecules and materials, is computationally expensive for classical computers. The number of variables required to accurately model these systems grows exponentially with their size. This limitation hinders advancements in fields like drug discovery, materials science, and chemical engineering.
  - For example, simulating the behavior of a complex protein or

designing new catalysts requires modeling the intricate interactions of countless atoms and electrons. Classical computers struggle to handle this complexity within a reasonable timeframe.

- **Optimization Problems:**
  - Many real-world problems, such as logistics, finance, and artificial intelligence, involve finding optimal solutions within a vast search space. Classical algorithms often rely on brute-force approaches or heuristics, which can be inefficient or fail to find the best solution.
  - Consider the traveling salesman problem, where the goal is to find the shortest route that visits a set of cities. As the number of cities increases, the computational complexity grows

exponentially, making it impractical for classical computers to find the optimal solution.

- **Cryptography:**
  - Modern encryption methods, such as RSA, rely on the difficulty of factoring large numbers.[2] However, Shor's algorithm, a quantum algorithm, can efficiently factor large numbers, posing a significant threat to current cryptographic systems.[3]
  - The need for quantum-resistant cryptography is becoming increasingly urgent as quantum computers become more powerful.[4]
- **Machine Learning and Artificial Intelligence:**
  - Classical machine learning algorithms can struggle with massive datasets and complex

patterns.[5] Quantum algorithms offer the potential to accelerate machine learning tasks, such as pattern recognition, data analysis, and optimization.[6]

- Quantum machine learning could revolutionize fields like image recognition, natural language processing, and personalized medicine.[7]

- **Financial Modeling:**
  - Financial modelling often relies on complex simulations of market behavior, which can be computationally intensive. Quantum computers have the potential to perform these simulations much more efficiently, leading to more accurate risk assessments and investment strategies.[8]

- **Materials Discovery:**
  - The discovery of new materials with specific properties is

essential for advancements in many industries. Quantum simulations can accelerate the design and discovery of new materials by accurately predicting their properties.[9]

1.2 Classical vs. Quantum Computing: A Paradigm Shift

The fundamental difference between classical and quantum computing lies in the way they represent and manipulate information.

- **Classical Computing:**
  - Classical computers operate on bits, which can exist in one of two states: 0 or 1.[10]

- Information is processed using logic gates, which perform deterministic operations on bits.[11]
- Classical computers follow the laws of classical physics.[12]
- The amount of information that a classical bit can store is limited to one of two states.[13]
- **Quantum Computing:**
  - Quantum computers operate on qubits, which can exist in a superposition of states, meaning they can be 0 and 1 simultaneously.[14]
  - Information is processed using quantum gates, which perform unitary operations on qubits.[15]
  - Quantum computers leverage the principles of quantum mechanics, such as superposition, entanglement, and interference.[16]

- A Qubit can hold exponentially more information than a classical bit.[17]
- **Superposition:**
  - A qubit can exist in a linear combination of the states $|0\rangle$ and $|1\rangle$, represented as $\alpha|0\rangle + \beta|1\rangle$, where α and β are complex numbers. This allows qubits to explore multiple possibilities simultaneously.
- **Entanglement:**
  - Entangled qubits are correlated in such a way that the state of one qubit instantaneously affects the state of the other, regardless of the distance between them.[18][19] This phenomenon enables powerful quantum algorithms.

- ○ **Interference:**
  - ■ Quantum interference allows us to manipulate the probabilities of different quantum states, amplifying desired outcomes and suppressing undesired ones.[20] This is a key mechanism in many quantum algorithms.

The Paradigm Shift:

- The shift from classical to quantum computing represents a paradigm shift in how we approach computation.[21] It's not just about building faster computers; it's about harnessing the fundamental laws of nature to perform computations that are impossible for classical machines.

- This shift necessitates a change in our thinking, moving from deterministic algorithms to probabilistic ones, and from classical logic to quantum logic.
- Quantum computing is not intended to replace classical computing entirely. Classical computers will continue to be essential for everyday tasks. Instead, quantum computers will complement classical computers, tackling problems that are beyond their reach.
- The development of quantum computing requires a multidisciplinary approach, bringing together expertise from physics, computer science, mathematics, and engineering.[22]

Educational Importance:

Understanding the need for quantum computing and the fundamental differences between classical and quantum computing is crucial for preparing the next generation of scientists, engineers, and technologists. As quantum computing matures, it will transform various industries and create new opportunities.[23] Education in quantum computing is essential for:

- Developing the workforce needed to build and operate quantum computers.
- Enabling researchers to develop new quantum algorithms and applications.
- Educating the public about the potential and implications of quantum technology.

By embracing this paradigm shift, we can unlock the immense potential of quantum computing and address some of the most challenging problems facing humanity.

1.3 Key Concepts: Superposition, Entanglement, and Interference – The Quantum Trinity

These three phenomena are the cornerstones of quantum computing, distinguishing it from classical computation and enabling its extraordinary potential.

- **Superposition:**
    - At the heart of quantum mechanics lies the principle of superposition, which states that a quantum system can exist in multiple states simultaneously.[1] Unlike a classical bit, which is confined to either 0 or 1, a qubit can be in a linear combination of these states.[2]
    - Mathematically, a qubit's state can be represented as $|\psi\rangle = \alpha|0\rangle + \beta|1\rangle$, where $|0\rangle$ and $|1\rangle$ are the basis states, and α and β are complex numbers representing

the probability amplitudes. The absolute squares of these amplitudes, $|\alpha|^2$ and $|\beta|^2$, give the probabilities of measuring the qubit in the $|0\rangle$ or $|1\rangle$ state, respectively.[3]

- Imagine a coin spinning in the air. Before it lands, it's neither heads nor tails, but a superposition of both. This is analogous to a qubit in superposition.
- Superposition allows quantum computers to explore a vast number of possibilities simultaneously, enabling them to perform computations that are intractable for classical computers.[4]

- **Entanglement:**
  - Entanglement is a peculiar phenomenon where two or more qubits become correlated in such a way that their fates are

intertwined.[5] Even when separated by vast distances, the state of one qubit instantaneously affects the state of the others.[6]

- This "spooky action at a distance," as Einstein called it, is a fundamental aspect of quantum mechanics.[7]
- When two qubits are entangled, their combined state cannot be described as a product of individual states.[8] Instead, they form a single, inseparable quantum state.
- Entanglement is crucial for many quantum algorithms, enabling tasks like quantum teleportation and quantum key distribution.[9]
- Imagine two gloves, one left and one right. If they are placed into two separate boxes, and you open one box and find the left

glove, you instantly know the other box contains the right glove. Entanglement works in a similar, but far more complex, way.

- **Interference:**
    - Quantum interference arises from the wave-like nature of quantum particles.[10] When multiple quantum states are superimposed, their probability amplitudes can interfere constructively or destructively.[11]
    - Constructive interference amplifies desired outcomes, while destructive interference cancels out undesired ones.[12] This allows quantum algorithms to manipulate probabilities and enhance the likelihood of finding the correct solution.
    - This is very similiar to how water waves can either amplify or cancel each other out.

- Interference is a key mechanism in algorithms like Grover's search algorithm and Shor's factoring algorithm.

1.4 Quantum Bits (Qubits) and Their Properties – The Quantum Information Carriers

Qubits are the fundamental units of information in quantum computing.[13] Unlike classical bits, which can only be 0 or 1, qubits can exist in a superposition of both states.[14]

- **Representation:**
  - Qubits are often represented using Dirac notation, where $|0\rangle$ and $|1\rangle$ denote the basis states.
  - The state of a qubit can be visualized using the Bloch sphere, a geometric representation where the north

and south poles correspond to $|0\rangle$ and $|1\rangle$, respectively, and any point on the sphere's surface represents a superposition state.[15]

- **Properties:**
  - **Superposition:** As discussed earlier, qubits can exist in a superposition of states.[16]
  - **Measurement:** When a qubit is measured, its superposition collapses into one of the basis states, $|0\rangle$ or $|1\rangle$.[17] The probability of measuring a particular state is determined by the square of the corresponding probability amplitude.
  - **Coherence:** Qubits are highly sensitive to their environment and can lose their superposition due to interactions with external factors.[18] This phenomenon is known as decoherence, and it poses a significant challenge for

building practical quantum computers.

- ○ **Manipulation:** Qubits can be manipulated using quantum gates, which perform unitary operations on their states.[19]

1.5 Quantum Gates: The Building Blocks of Quantum Circuits – The Quantum Logic Operators

Quantum gates are the quantum equivalent of classical logic gates.[20] They are unitary operators that manipulate the states of qubits.[21]

- • **Types of Quantum Gates:**
  - ○ **Pauli Gates (X, Y, Z):** These gates perform rotations around the x, y, and z axes of the Bloch sphere.[22]

- **Hadamard Gate (H):** This gate creates an equal superposition of $|0\rangle$ and $|1\rangle$.[23]
- **Phase Gate (S, T):** These gates introduce a phase shift to the qubit's state.[24]
- **Controlled Gates (CNOT, CZ):** These gates perform operations on target qubits based on the state of control qubits, enabling entanglement.[25]
- **Rotation Gates (Rx, Ry, Rz):** These gates perform rotations around the x, y, and z axes by arbitrary angles.[26]
- **Universal Quantum Gates:** Any quantum computation can be performed using a combination of a small set of universal quantum gates.[27] A common set is the Hadamard gate, the phase gate, and the CNOT gate.[28]
- **Quantum Circuits:**

- Quantum circuits are sequences of quantum gates applied to qubits.[29] They are used to implement quantum algorithms.
- Quantum circuits are typically represented using diagrams, where horizontal lines represent qubits and boxes represent quantum gates.[30]
- Reading a quantum circuit is done from left to right.[31]

- **Importance:**
  - Quantum gates are essential for manipulating qubits and implementing quantum algorithms.[32]
  - The ability to design and control quantum gates is crucial for building practical quantum computers.
  - The creation of less error prone gates is a large part of current quantum computing research.[33]

By understanding these fundamental concepts, we can begin to appreciate the power and potential of quantum computing. These concepts are not just theoretical curiosities; they are the building blocks of a new era of computation that promises to revolutionize science, technology, and society.

1.6 Applications of Quantum Computing: Unlocking New Frontiers

Quantum computing's potential to revolutionize numerous fields stems from its ability to tackle problems that are intractable for classical computers.[1] Here are some of the most promising areas of application:

- **Drug Discovery and Materials Science:**
    - Quantum computers can simulate the behavior of

molecules and materials with unprecedented accuracy, accelerating the discovery of new drugs and materials.[2]

- o Simulating molecular interactions can help researchers understand protein folding, design new catalysts, and develop novel pharmaceuticals.[3]
- o In materials science, quantum simulations can predict the properties of new materials, leading to the development of stronger, lighter, and more efficient materials for various applications.[4]

- **Optimization:**
  - o Many real-world problems involve finding optimal solutions within a vast search space. Quantum optimization algorithms, such as the Quantum Approximate

Optimization Algorithm (QAOA), can potentially solve these problems more efficiently than classical algorithms.[5]

- Applications include:
  - Logistics and supply chain optimization: Finding the most efficient routes for delivery trucks or optimizing resource allocation.[6]
  - Financial portfolio optimization: Maximizing returns while minimizing risk.[7]
  - Traffic flow optimization: Reducing congestion and improving transportation efficiency.[8]
- **Cryptography:**
  - While quantum computers pose a threat to current encryption methods, they also offer the

potential for more secure communication.[9]

○ Quantum key distribution (QKD) uses the principles of quantum mechanics to generate and distribute encryption keys that are provably secure.[10]

○ Post-quantum cryptography research is focused on developing encryption algorithms that are resistant to attacks from both classical and quantum computers.[11]

- **Artificial Intelligence and Machine Learning:**
  ○ Quantum machine learning algorithms can potentially accelerate tasks such as pattern recognition, data analysis, and optimization.[12]

  ○ Quantum computers can handle massive datasets and complex patterns more efficiently than classical computers, leading to breakthroughs in areas like image recognition, natural language processing, and personalized medicine.[13]

- o Variational Quantum Eigensolvers are being explored for machine learning tasks.[14]

- **Financial Modeling:**
  - o Quantum computers can perform complex financial simulations more efficiently than classical computers, leading to more accurate risk assessments and investment strategies.[15]
  - o Applications include:
    - Pricing derivatives and other financial instruments.[16]
    - Detecting fraud and other financial anomalies.[17]
    - Optimizing trading strategies.

- **Quantum Simulation of Physical Systems:**
  - Quantum computers are uniquely suited to simulating other quantum systems.[18] This ability is incredibly useful for understanding the behavior of complex physical phenomena.
  - This is applicable to high energy physics, and better understanding of the universe.
  - This is also applicable to understanding how the human brain works.

1.7 The Current State and Future of Quantum Technology: A Rapidly Evolving Landscape

Quantum technology is still in its early stages of development, but it is advancing rapidly.[19]

- **Current State:**
  - Researchers have built small-scale quantum computers with a limited number of qubits.[20]
  - Several different qubit technologies are being explored, including superconducting qubits, trapped ions, and photonic qubits.
  - Quantum cloud platforms are emerging, allowing researchers and developers to access quantum computers remotely.[21]
  - Noise and decoherence are still major obstacles to building large-scale, fault-tolerant quantum computers.[22]
  - The Noisy Intermediate-Scale Quantum (NISQ) era is the current state, where quantum computers can perform some tasks, but are still very susceptible to errors.[23]

- **Future of Quantum Technology:**
  - The goal is to build large-scale, fault-tolerant quantum computers that can solve complex problems beyond the reach of classical computers.[24]
  - Quantum computing is expected to have a transformative impact on various industries, creating new opportunities and challenges.[25]
  - The development of quantum technology requires a multidisciplinary approach, bringing together expertise from physics, computer science, mathematics, and engineering.[26]
  - Quantum internet and quantum communication networks are being developed, to allow for secure quantum information transfer.[27]
  - Error correction is a very large focus of current research, as that

is the key to scaling up the amount of useable qubits.[28]
- Hybrid quantum-classical algorithms are expected to be very important in the near future.
- Quantum sensors are being developed, that will allow for extremely accurate measurements.[29]

Challenges and Opportunities:

- **Challenges:**
  - Building and scaling up quantum computers is a complex engineering challenge.
  - Developing quantum algorithms and software requires specialized expertise.[30]
  - Addressing the ethical and societal implications of quantum technology is crucial.

- **Opportunities:**
  - Quantum computing has the potential to solve some of the most challenging problems facing humanity.[31]
  - It can drive innovation in various industries and create new economic opportunities.[32]
  - Investing in quantum education and research is essential for realizing the full potential of this technology.

Quantum technology is poised to revolutionize the 21st century.[33] By understanding its applications and the challenges and opportunities it presents, we can prepare for a future where quantum computing plays a central role in science, technology, and society.

CHAPTER 2

Mathematical Preliminaries for Quantum Computing

Quantum computing, by its very nature, is deeply rooted in mathematics.[1] To understand the behaviors of qubits, quantum gates, and quantum algorithms, a solid grasp of certain mathematical concepts is indispensable. Linear algebra, complex numbers, and Dirac notation form the bedrock upon which the entire edifice of quantum computation is built.

2.1 Linear Algebra: Vectors, Matrices, and Complex Numbers – The Foundation of Quantum Operations

Linear algebra provides the framework for representing and manipulating quantum states and operations.[2]

- **Vectors:**
    - In quantum computing, vectors are used to represent the states of qubits.[3] A qubit's state, such as $|0\rangle$ or $|1\rangle$, can be expressed as a vector in a two-dimensional complex vector space.[4]
    - For instance, the state $|0\rangle$ can be represented as the vector $[1, 0]^T$, and $|1\rangle$ as $[0, 1]^T$.
    - Superposition states are represented by linear combinations of these basis vectors.
    - The concept of vector spaces allows us to understand the possible states of qubits and how they evolve.[5]
- **Matrices:**

- Quantum gates, the building blocks of quantum circuits, are represented by matrices.[6] These matrices are typically unitary, meaning they preserve the norm of vectors.[7]
- Unitary matrices are crucial because they ensure that quantum operations are reversible, a fundamental requirement of quantum mechanics.[8]
- Matrix multiplication is used to represent the application of quantum gates to qubits.[9]
- For example, the Hadamard gate, which creates a superposition, is represented by a 2x2 matrix.[10]
- Eigenvalues and eigenvectors of matrices are also important for understanding the properties of quantum gates and the

outcomes of quantum measurements.

- **Complex Numbers:**
  - Quantum mechanics, and therefore quantum computing, relies heavily on complex numbers.[11]
  - The probability amplitudes of quantum states are complex numbers, and their absolute squares give the probabilities of measurement outcomes.[12]
  - Complex numbers allow us to represent the phase of quantum states, which plays a crucial role in quantum interference.
  - The phase of a quantum state is a critical factor in quantum interference, a phenomenon that allows quantum computers to perform computations that are impossible for classical computers.[13]

- The complex conjugate is used in the calculation of probabilities.
- The use of complex numbers allows for a much more complete description of the quantum state than real numbers would allow.

2.2 Dirac Notation: A Quantum Mechanic's Language – Simplifying Quantum Expressions

Dirac notation, also known as bra-ket notation, is a convenient and powerful way to represent quantum states and operations.[14]

- **Ket Notation ($|\psi\rangle$):**
  - A ket $|\psi\rangle$ represents a column vector, or a quantum state.[15]

- For example, $|0\rangle$ and $|1\rangle$ represent the basis states of a qubit.
- The superposition state $\alpha|0\rangle + \beta|1\rangle$ represents a linear combination of the basis states.[16]

- **Bra Notation ($\langle\psi|$):**
  - A bra $\langle\psi|$ represents a row vector, which is the conjugate transpose of the corresponding ket vector.
  - The bra $\langle\psi|$ is used to represent the dual vector of $|\psi\rangle$.

- **Bra-Ket Notation ($\langle\psi|\varphi\rangle$):**
  - The inner product of two quantum states $|\psi\rangle$ and $|\varphi\rangle$ is represented by $\langle\psi|\varphi\rangle$.
  - This notation simplifies the representation of inner products and other linear algebra operations.[17]
  - The inner product allows for the calculation of the overlap between two quantum states.

- **Outer Product ($|\psi\rangle\langle\varphi|$):**
  - The outer product is used to represent linear operators.
  - This is used to construct projection operators.
- **Advantages of Dirac Notation:**
  - It simplifies the representation of quantum states and operations, making it easier to write and manipulate quantum equations.
  - It provides a concise and elegant way to express concepts such as superposition, entanglement, and measurement.[18]
  - It is widely used in quantum mechanics and quantum computing literature, making it essential for understanding and communicating quantum ideas.[19]

Educational Importance:

A strong foundation in linear algebra, complex numbers, and Dirac notation is essential for anyone interested in quantum computing. These mathematical tools provide the language and framework for understanding and developing quantum algorithms and applications. By mastering these concepts, you can unlock the power of quantum computing and contribute to the advancement of this transformative technology.

2.3 Tensor Products and Multi-Qubit Systems: Building Larger Quantum States

In quantum computing, we often work with multiple qubits.[1] The tensor product is the mathematical tool that allows us to combine the states of individual qubits to form the state of a multi-qubit system.

- **Understanding the Tensor Product:**
  - The tensor product, denoted by $\otimes$, is a way of multiplying vector spaces to create a larger vector space.[2]
  - If we have two qubits, one in state $|\psi\rangle$ and the other in state $|\varphi\rangle$, their combined state is represented by $|\psi\rangle \otimes |\varphi\rangle$.
  - For example, if $|\psi\rangle = \alpha|0\rangle + \beta|1\rangle$ and $|\varphi\rangle = \gamma|0\rangle + \delta|1\rangle$, then:
    - $|\psi\rangle \otimes |\varphi\rangle = \alpha\gamma|00\rangle + \alpha\delta|01\rangle + \beta\gamma|10\rangle + \beta\delta|11\rangle$.
  - The resulting state is a vector in a four-dimensional space, representing the four possible states of the two-qubit system: $|00\rangle$, $|01\rangle$, $|10\rangle$, and $|11\rangle$.
  - The size of the resulting vector space grows exponentially with the number of qubits. This exponential growth is a key feature of quantum computing,

allowing quantum computers to represent and manipulate vast amounts of information.

- **Multi-Qubit Systems:**
  - The tensor product allows us to describe the states of multi-qubit systems, which are essential for performing complex quantum computations.[3]
  - For a system of n qubits, the state space has dimension 2^n.[4]
  - Entangled states, such as the Bell states, are examples of multi-qubit states that cannot be expressed as a product of individual qubit states.[5]
  - Understanding tensor products is essential for constructing and analyzing quantum circuits that operate on multiple qubits.[6]
  - Tensor products also play a vital role in understanding how

quantum gates operate on multiple qubits.[7]

2.4 Probability and Statistics in Quantum Computing: Dealing with Uncertainty

Quantum mechanics is inherently probabilistic.[8] When we measure a qubit, we don't get a deterministic outcome; instead, we get a probabilistic outcome determined by the quantum state.

- **Probabilities in Quantum Measurement:**
  - The probability of measuring a qubit in a particular state is given by the square of the magnitude of the corresponding probability amplitude.[9]
  - For example, if a qubit is in the state $\alpha|0\rangle + \beta|1\rangle$, the probability of measuring $|0\rangle$ is $|\alpha|^2$, and the

probability of measuring $|1\rangle$ is $|\beta|^2$.

- In multi-qubit systems, the probabilities are calculated similarly, but the probability amplitudes are associated with the basis states of the multi-qubit system.

- **Statistical Analysis:**
  - Because quantum measurements are probabilistic, we need to perform statistical analysis to obtain meaningful results.
  - We often repeat quantum measurements multiple times to estimate the probabilities of different outcomes.[10]
  - Statistical tools, such as mean, variance, and standard deviation, are used to analyze the results of quantum measurements.

- The use of statistics is essential for characterizing the performance of quantum algorithms and for quantifying the effects of noise and errors.[11]
- Sampling from probability distributions created by quantum circuits is a key component of many quantum algorithms.[12]

- **Applications:**
  - Probability and statistics are fundamental to quantum machine learning, where quantum algorithms are used to learn from probabilistic data.[13]
  - They are also crucial in quantum error correction, where statistical methods are used to detect and correct errors in quantum computations.[14]

2.5 Quantum Measurement and its Mathematical Representation: Extracting Information

Quantum measurement is the process of extracting classical information from a quantum system. It is a crucial step in any quantum computation.

- **Measurement Process:**
    - When a quantum measurement is performed, the quantum state collapses into one of the basis states.[15]
    - The outcome of the measurement is probabilistic, determined by the probabilities associated with the basis states.
    - The measurement process is irreversible, meaning that the original quantum state is destroyed.
- **Mathematical Representation:**

- Quantum measurements are mathematically represented by measurement operators.[16]
- A measurement operator is a Hermitian operator that corresponds to a particular measurement outcome.[17]
- The probability of obtaining a particular measurement outcome is given by the expectation value of the corresponding measurement operator.
- Projective measurements are a standard type of measurement that project a quantum state onto a basis state.[18]
- Generalized measurements, or POVMs (Positive Operator-Valued Measures), provide a more general framework for describing quantum measurements.[19]

- The measurement operator is used to calculate the probability of each outcome.[20]
- The collapse of the wavefunction is mathematically represented by the application of the measurement operator.

- **Importance:**
  - Quantum measurement is essential for extracting the results of quantum computations.[21]
  - It is also used in quantum communication and quantum sensing.
  - Understanding the mathematical representation of quantum measurement is crucial for designing and analyzing quantum algorithms and applications.

By mastering these mathematical concepts, you gain the ability to fully understand how multi-qubit systems function, how to interpret the results of quantum computations, and how to effectively design and implement quantum algorithms. These concepts are the key to unlocking the power of quantum information processing.

CHAPTER 3

Introduction to Quantum Algorithms: Harnessing Quantum Power

Quantum algorithms are the heart of quantum computing, providing the instructions that leverage the unique capabilities of qubits to solve problems that are intractable for classical computers.[1] They represent a fundamental shift in computational thinking, moving from classical, deterministic approaches to probabilistic, quantum-enhanced methods.[2]

3.1 Quantum Algorithm Design Principles: Crafting Quantum Solutions

Designing effective quantum algorithms requires a deep understanding of quantum mechanics and a creative approach to problem-solving.[3] Here are some key principles that guide the development of quantum algorithms:

- **Exploiting Superposition:**
  - Quantum algorithms leverage superposition to explore multiple possibilities simultaneously.[4] This allows them to perform computations on a vast number of inputs at once, leading to exponential speedups in certain cases.[5]
  - The ability to manipulate probability amplitudes in superposition is crucial for amplifying desired outcomes and suppressing undesired ones.
- **Harnessing Entanglement:**
  - Entanglement allows for the creation of correlations between qubits, enabling complex

computations that are impossible for classical systems.[6]
- Entangled states can be used to perform tasks like quantum teleportation and quantum key distribution.[7]
- Entanglement is a key resource for quantum error correction.[8]

- **Leveraging Quantum Interference:**
  - Quantum interference allows us to manipulate the probabilities of different quantum states.[9]
  - By carefully designing quantum circuits, we can create constructive interference for desired outcomes and destructive interference for undesired ones.[10]
  - This is the core mechanism behind algorithms like Grover's search and Shor's factoring.

- **Quantum Fourier Transform (QFT):**

- The QFT is a quantum analogue of the classical discrete Fourier transform.[11]
- It is a fundamental building block of many quantum algorithms, including Shor's algorithm and quantum phase estimation.[12]
- The QFT enables efficient manipulation of quantum states in the frequency domain.[13]

- **Variational Quantum Algorithms:**
  - These hybrid quantum-classical algorithms use a classical computer to optimize the parameters of a quantum circuit.
  - They are particularly useful for problems in quantum chemistry, materials science, and optimization.[14]
  - Examples include the Variational Quantum Eigensolver (VQE) and the

Quantum   Approximate
Optimization   Algorithm
(QAOA).[15]

- **Quantum Phase Estimation:**
  - This algorithm is used to estimate the eigenvalues of a unitary operator.
  - It is a core component of Shor's algorithm, and many quantum simulation algorithms.
- **Circuit Depth and Complexity:**
  - The number of quantum gates and the depth of the quantum circuit are critical factors in determining the efficiency and feasibility of a quantum algorithm.[16]
  - Minimizing circuit depth and complexity is essential for implementing quantum algorithms on near-term quantum devices.[17]
- **Error Mitigation and Correction:**

- Quantum computers are susceptible to noise and errors.[18]
- Quantum error correction techniques are essential for building fault-tolerant quantum computers.[19]
- Error mitigation techniques are used to reduce the impact of noise on quantum computations.[20]

3.2 Grover's Search Algorithm: Finding Needles in Haystacks – A Quantum Speedup

Grover's algorithm is a quantum algorithm that provides a quadratic speedup for unstructured search problems.[21]

- **The Search Problem:**
  - Imagine you have a list of N items, and you want to find a

specific item that satisfies a certain condition.

- ○ In the classical world, you would have to check each item one by one, which would take $O(N)$ time in the worst case.

- **Grover's Algorithm Approach:**
  - ○ Grover's algorithm uses quantum superposition and interference to find the target item in $O(\sqrt{N})$ time.[22]
  - ○ It involves two main steps:
    - ■ **Oracle Query:** An oracle is used to mark the target item.[23] This is a quantum function that recognizes the solution.
    - ■ **Amplitude Amplification:** This step amplifies the probability amplitude of the target item, while suppressing the amplitudes of the other items.[24]

- **Algorithm Steps:**
  - **Initialization:** Start with an equal superposition of all possible states.
  - **Oracle Application:** Apply the oracle to mark the target item.
  - **Amplitude Inversion:** Invert the amplitudes of all states about their average.
  - **Repeat:** Repeat steps 2 and 3 approximately $\sqrt{N}$ times.[25]
  - **Measurement:** Measure the quantum state to obtain the target item.
- **Key Features:**
  - Quadratic speedup: Grover's algorithm provides a significant speedup over classical search algorithms.[26]
  - Unstructured search: It works for any unstructured search problem, where there is no known structure or order to the items.[27]

- Probabilistic algorithm: The algorithm provides a high probability of finding the target item, but it is not guaranteed to find it in every run.[28]
- **Applications:**
  - Database searching: Finding specific records in a large database.
  - Optimization problems: Finding optimal solutions in a search space.[29]
  - Cryptography: Breaking certain types of cryptographic keys.
  - Solving NP-complete problems, with a quadratic speed up compared to classical methods.

Educational Importance:

Understanding quantum algorithms is essential for realizing the full potential of quantum computing. By mastering the design principles and studying algorithms like Grover's, you can contribute to the development of new quantum applications and help shape the future of computation.

3.3 Shor's Factoring Algorithm: Breaking Classical Cryptography – A Quantum Threat and a Mathematical Marvel

Shor's algorithm is a quantum algorithm that can efficiently factor large numbers, a task that is believed to be computationally intractable for classical computers.[1] This capability has significant implications for cryptography, as many widely used encryption methods rely on the difficulty of factoring large numbers.[2]

- **The Factoring Problem:**
    - Given a large composite number N, the goal is to find its prime factors.[3]

- Classical algorithms, such as the general number field sieve, take exponential time to factor large numbers.[4]
- The security of widely used cryptographic systems, such as RSA, relies on the assumption that factoring large numbers is computationally difficult.[5]

- **Shor's Algorithm Approach:**
  - Shor's algorithm uses the Quantum Fourier Transform (QFT) and quantum phase estimation to efficiently find the period of a function related to the factoring problem.[6]
  - The period can then be used to determine the prime factors of N.

- **Algorithm Steps:**
  - **Classical Preprocessing:** Choose a random number less than N.
  - **Quantum Period Finding:**

- Create a superposition of all possible values of x.
- Apply a quantum function that maps x to a^x mod N.
- Use the QFT to find the period r of the function.
  - **Classical Postprocessing:**
    - If r is even and a^(r/2) mod N is not -1, then gcd(a^(r/2) ± 1, N) are nontrivial factors of N.
    - If the conditions are not met, repeat the algorithm with a different random a.

- **Key Features:**
  - Exponential speedup: Shor's algorithm provides an exponential speedup over classical factoring algorithms.[7]
  - Impact on cryptography: It poses a significant threat to widely used public-key encryption methods.[8]

- Mathematical elegance: The algorithm combines concepts from number theory, quantum mechanics, and Fourier analysis.[9]
- **Implications:**
  - The development of quantum-resistant cryptography is crucial for ensuring secure communication in the quantum era.[10]
  - Shor's algorithm highlights the potential of quantum computers to break classical cryptographic systems.[11]
  - It also shows the power of quantum algorithms to solve problems that are intractable for classical computers.

3.4 Quantum Fourier Transform and Its Applications: A Versatile Tool

The Quantum Fourier Transform (QFT) is a quantum analogue of the classical discrete Fourier transform.[12] It is a fundamental building block of many quantum algorithms, including Shor's algorithm and quantum phase estimation.[13]

- **Understanding the QFT:**
    - The QFT transforms a quantum state from the computational basis to the frequency basis.
    - It is a unitary operation that can be implemented efficiently on a quantum computer.[14]
    - The QFT is used to find the periodicities within a quantum state.
- **Applications:**
    - **Shor's Algorithm:** The QFT is a core component of Shor's

algorithm, used to find the period of a function related to the factoring problem.

- **Quantum Phase Estimation:** The QFT is used to estimate the eigenvalues of a unitary operator, which is essential for many quantum simulation algorithms.[15]
- **Quantum Signal Processing:** The QFT can be used to perform quantum signal processing tasks, such as filtering and compression.[16]
- **Quantum Amplitude Estimation:** the QFT is used to estimate the amplitude of a specific quantum state.

- **Educational Importance:**
  - Understanding the QFT is essential for grasping the workings of many quantum algorithms.

- It demonstrates the power of quantum computing to perform tasks that are difficult for classical computers.[17]
- It highlights the connection between quantum mechanics and Fourier analysis.[18]

3.5 Quantum Simulation and Optimization Algorithms: Tackling Complex Problems

Quantum simulation and optimization algorithms are powerful tools for solving complex problems in various fields, including materials science, chemistry, and optimization.[19]

- **Quantum Simulation:**
  - Quantum computers are uniquely suited to simulating other quantum systems.[20]

- They can be used to model the behavior of molecules, materials, and other complex systems.[21]
- Applications include:
  - Drug discovery: Simulating molecular interactions to design new drugs.[22]
  - Materials science: Predicting the properties of new materials.
  - Quantum chemistry: Calculating the electronic structure of molecules.
- Variational Quantum Eigensolver (VQE) is a common algorithm used in this space.
- **Quantum Optimization:**
  - Many real-world problems involve finding optimal solutions within a vast search space.
  - Quantum optimization algorithms, such as the

Quantum Approximate Optimization Algorithm (QAOA), can potentially solve these problems more efficiently than classical algorithms.[23]

- Applications include:
    - Logistics and supply chain optimization.
    - Financial portfolio optimization.
    - Traffic flow optimization.
- QAOA is a hybrid quantum classical algorithm.[24]

- **Educational Importance:**
    - Quantum simulation and optimization algorithms have the potential to revolutionize various industries.
    - They demonstrate the power of quantum computing to tackle complex problems that are intractable for classical computers.

- They highlight the interdisciplinary nature of quantum computing, bringing together concepts from physics, computer science, and mathematics.[25]

By understanding these powerful quantum algorithms, we can appreciate the transformative potential of quantum computing and its ability to address some of the most challenging problems facing humanity.

Part II:

Python and Quantum Computing Frameworks

CHAPTER 4

Setting Up Your Quantum Programming Environment

Before diving into the exciting world of quantum algorithms and applications, it's crucial to establish a robust and efficient programming environment. This involves installing the necessary software, libraries, and tools that will enable you to write, simulate, and potentially run quantum programs on actual hardware.

4.1 Installing Python and Essential Libraries: The Base of Your Quantum Toolkit

Python has become the de facto language for quantum computing due to its versatility, readability, and extensive ecosystem of libraries.[1] Here's a comprehensive guide to setting up your Python environment:

- **Python Installation:**
  - **Download and Install:** Visit the official Python website (python.org) and download the latest stable version of Python for your operating system (Windows, macOS, or Linux).[2]
  - **Installation Process:** Follow the installation instructions carefully. On Windows, make sure to check the "Add Python to PATH" option during installation. This allows you to run Python from the command line.
  - **Verify Installation:** Open a terminal or command prompt and type `python --version` or `python3 --version`. This should display the installed Python version.

- **Virtual Environments (Recommended):**
  - **Purpose:** Virtual environments create isolated Python environments, preventing conflicts between different projects and their dependencies.[3]
  - **Installation:** If you don't have it already, Install the virtual enviroment package by typing pip install virtualenv into your terminal.
  - **Creation:** Create a virtual environment by navigating to your project directory and running virtualenv venv (or python3 -m venv venv).
  - **Activation:** Activate the virtual environment using venv\Scripts\activate (Windows) or source venv/bin/activate (macOS/Linux).

- **Essential Libraries:**
  - **NumPy:** NumPy is a fundamental library for numerical computing in Python.[4] It provides support for arrays, matrices, and mathematical functions,[5] which are essential for quantum computing. Install it using pip install numpy.
  - **SciPy:** SciPy is a library for scientific computing that builds on NumPy.[6] It provides a wide range of functions for optimization, integration, linear algebra, and more. Install it using pip install scipy.
  - **Matplotlib:** Matplotlib is a library for creating visualizations in Python.[7] It is used to plot quantum circuit diagrams, simulation results, and other data. Install it using pip install matplotlib.

- IPython/Jupyter: IPython is an interactive Python shell, and Jupyter Notebook is a web-based environment for creating and sharing documents that contain live code, equations, visualizations, and narrative text.[8] Jupyter[9] Notebook is especially useful for exploring and experimenting with quantum algorithms. Install them using `pip install ipython jupyter`.
- **Pip:** Python's package installer.[10] Make sure pip is up to date by running `python -m pip install --upgrade pip`

4.2 Introduction to Qiskit: IBM's Quantum Computing Framework – Your Gateway to Quantum Circuits

Qiskit (Quantum Information Science Kit) is an open-source software development kit (SDK) for working with quantum computers.[11] Developed by IBM, Qiskit provides tools for creating, manipulating, and simulating quantum circuits, and for running them on real quantum hardware.[12]

- **Qiskit Installation:**
  - Install Qiskit using pip install qiskit. This will install the core Qiskit components, including:
    - qiskit-terra: The base component for quantum circuits.
    - qiskit-aer: A high-performance quantum circuit simulator.

- ■ qiskit-ignis: Tools for noise characterization and error mitigation.
- ■ qiskit-aqua: Libraries for quantum algorithms and applications.
- **Qiskit Architecture:**
  - ○ **Terra:** Forms the foundation of Qiskit, providing tools for constructing quantum circuits, managing qubits and classical bits, and defining quantum gates.[13]
  - ○ **Aer:** Provides high-performance simulators that allow you to run quantum circuits locally.[14] Aer supports various simulation methods, including statevector simulation, unitary simulation, and noise simulation.[15]
  - ○ **Ignis:** Focuses on noise characterization and error mitigation. It provides tools for calibrating quantum devices,

characterizing noise sources, and applying error correction techniques.

- **Aqua:** Contains libraries for implementing quantum algorithms and applications in areas such as chemistry, optimization, and machine learning.[16]

- **Basic Qiskit Workflow:**
  - **Creating a Quantum Circuit:** Use Qiskit's QuantumCircuit class to create a quantum circuit.
  - **Adding Quantum Gates:** Add quantum gates to the circuit using methods like h(), x(), cx(), and measure().
  - **Simulating the Circuit:** Use Qiskit's Aer simulator to run the circuit and obtain the results.
  - **Visualizing the Circuit:** Use Qiskit's draw() method to visualize the quantum circuit.

- ○ **Running on Real Hardware (Optional):** If you have access to IBM Quantum hardware, you can run your circuits on real quantum computers.
- **Key Qiskit Features:**
  - ○ **Quantum Circuit Composer:** A graphical user interface for creating and visualizing quantum circuits.[17]
  - ○ **Qiskit Runtime:** A service for executing quantum programs on IBM Quantum hardware.[18]
  - ○ **Qiskit Textbook:** A comprehensive online resource for learning Qiskit and quantum computing.
  - ○ **Open-Source and Community-Driven:** Qiskit is an open-source project with a vibrant community of developers and users.[19]

Educational Importance:

Setting up a proper quantum programming environment is the first step towards exploring the fascinating world of quantum computing. By installing Python, essential libraries, and Qiskit, you'll be equipped to write, simulate, and potentially run quantum programs, laying the groundwork for your quantum journey.

4.3 Introduction to Cirq: Google's Quantum Computing Framework – A Flexible and Powerful Tool

Cirq is Google's open-source framework for programming quantum computers.[1] It's designed to be flexible, allowing researchers and developers to easily experiment with and explore quantum algorithms and hardware.[2] Cirq emphasizes noise modeling and hardware-aware compilation, making it particularly useful for developing applications for near-term quantum devices.[3]

- **Cirq's Design Philosophy:**
  - **Flexibility:** Cirq is designed to be highly flexible, allowing users to define custom gates, devices, and noise models.[4]
  - **Hardware Awareness:** Cirq provides tools for compiling quantum circuits to specific hardware architectures, taking into account the limitations and capabilities of real quantum devices.[5]
  - **Noise Modeling:** Cirq supports detailed noise modeling, allowing users to simulate the effects of noise on quantum computations.[6]
  - **Focus on NISQ:** Cirq is particularly well-suited for developing applications for

Noisy Intermediate-Scale Quantum (NISQ) devices.[7]

- **Cirq's Architecture:**
  - **Circuits:** Cirq uses a Circuit object to represent quantum circuits. Circuits are composed of Operations, which can be gates, measurements, or other instructions.
  - **Devices:** Cirq provides abstractions for quantum devices, representing the physical layout and connectivity of qubits.
  - **Gates:** Cirq includes a library of standard quantum gates, as well as tools for defining custom gates.[8]
  - **Simulators:** Cirq provides high-performance simulators for running quantum circuits.[9]
  - **Compilers:** Cirq includes compilers for optimizing

quantum circuits for specific hardware architectures.[10]

- **Basic Cirq Workflow:**
  - **Defining Qubits:** Create Qubit objects to represent the qubits in your circuit.
  - **Creating a Circuit:** Create a Circuit object to represent your quantum circuit.
  - **Adding Gates:** Add gates to the circuit using methods like cirq.H, cirq.X, and cirq.CNOT.
  - **Adding Measurements:** Add measurements to the circuit using cirq.measure.
  - **Simulating the Circuit:** Use Cirq's simulators to run the circuit and obtain the results.[11]
  - **Visualizing the Circuit:** Cirq allows you to visualize your circuit.[12]
- **Key Cirq Features:**
  - **Parametrized Circuits:** Cirq supports parametrized circuits,

which are essential for variational quantum algorithms.[13]

- **Noise Models:** Cirq provides tools for defining and applying noise models to quantum circuits.[14]
- **Hardware-Aware Compilation:** Cirq includes compilers for optimizing quantum circuits for specific hardware architectures.[15]
- **Open-Source and Community-Driven:** Cirq is an open-source project with a vibrant community of developers and users.[16]

4.4 Setting Up Local Simulators: Your Quantum Playground

Local simulators are essential for developing and testing quantum algorithms without requiring access to real quantum hardware. They provide a cost-effective and convenient way to experiment with quantum circuits.

- **Qiskit Aer:**
  - Qiskit Aer is a high-performance quantum circuit simulator that is part of the Qiskit SDK.[17]
  - It supports various simulation methods, including statevector simulation, unitary simulation, and noise simulation.[18]
  - Aer is highly optimized and can simulate relatively large quantum circuits efficiently.
  - Using Aer is as simple as importing the Aer module, and selecting a backend.
- **Cirq Simulator:**
  - Cirq includes its own simulator, which is integrated with the framework.[19]
  - The Cirq simulator is designed to be flexible and extensible,

allowing users to customize simulation parameters and noise models.

- Cirq also allows for simulation of noisy circuits.[20]
- **Benefits of Local Simulators:**
  - **Accessibility:** Local simulators are readily available and easy to use.
  - **Cost-Effectiveness:** They eliminate the need for expensive access to real quantum hardware.
  - **Rapid Prototyping:** They allow for rapid prototyping and testing of quantum algorithms.
  - **Debugging:** They provide tools for debugging and analyzing quantum circuits.
- **Limitations of Local Simulators:**
  - **Scalability:** Local simulators are limited by the computational resources of the host computer.

- ○ **Accuracy:** They may not accurately simulate the behavior of real quantum hardware, especially in the presence of noise.
- ○ **Real Hardware Characteristics:** Local simulators can not perfectly replicate the noise, and other unique characteristics of real quantum hardware.

4.5 Connecting to Quantum Hardware (IBM Quantum Experience, Google Quantum Cloud): Bridging the Gap to Reality

Connecting to real quantum hardware is the ultimate goal of quantum computing. It allows you to run your quantum programs on actual quantum devices and explore the limitations and capabilities of current quantum technology.

- **IBM Quantum Experience:**
    - The IBM Quantum Experience provides access to IBM's quantum computers through the cloud.[21]
    - It offers a graphical user interface (Quantum Composer) and a Python SDK (Qiskit) for creating and running quantum circuits.
    - IBM Quantum provides access to a range of quantum devices with varying numbers of qubits and connectivity.[22]
    - IBM quantum also provides real time information about the status of their machines.[23]
- **Google Quantum Cloud:**
    - Google Quantum Cloud provides access to Google's quantum

computers and simulators through the cloud.[24]

- It offers a Python SDK (Cirq) for creating and running quantum circuits.[25]
- Google Quantum Cloud also provides access to their quantum computing API's.[26]

- **Connecting and Executing:**
  - Both IBM Quantum Experience and Google Quantum Cloud require an account and API key to access their services.
  - Once you have an account and API key, you can use the respective Python SDKs to connect to the quantum hardware and execute your quantum circuits.
  - The results of the quantum computations are returned to your computer, allowing you to analyze and interpret them.[27]
- **Considerations:**

- **Queue Times:** Access to real quantum hardware is often limited, so you may experience queue times.
- **Noise and Errors:** Real quantum devices are susceptible to noise and errors, which can affect the accuracy of your results.[28]
- **Calibration:** Real quantum hardware requires regular calibration to maintain its performance.[29]

- **Educational Importance:**
  - Connecting to real quantum hardware provides invaluable experience in working with quantum devices.
  - It allows you to explore the limitations and capabilities of current quantum technology.
  - It provides a glimpse into the future of quantum computing.

By mastering these skills, you'll be well-equipped to explore the exciting world of quantum computing, from developing and testing quantum algorithms to running them on real quantum hardware.

CHAPTER 5

Qiskit: Building and Simulating Quantum Circuits

Qiskit: Building and Simulating Quantum Circuits – From Abstraction to Implementation (Enhanced)

Qiskit is not just a tool; it's a bridge between theoretical quantum concepts and practical quantum programming. Let's explore how to effectively utilize Qiskit to build and simulate quantum circuits, emphasizing real-world relevance and educational depth.

5.1 Working with Qubits and Classical Registers in Qiskit: The Foundation of Quantum Information (Practical Application Focus)

- Qubits – More Than Just Bits:
    - Think of QuantumRegister as your canvas. Each qubit within it is a brushstroke waiting to create a quantum masterpiece.
    - Practical Example: Imagine simulating a simple quantum coin toss. You'd need a single qubit.
    - Python

from qiskit import QuantumRegister, ClassicalRegister, QuantumCircuit

```
qr = QuantumRegister(1, 'coin')  # Naming
the register for clarity
cr = ClassicalRegister(1, 'outcome')
circuit = QuantumCircuit(qr, cr)
```

- ○
- ○
  - ○ Educational Insight: Emphasize that qubits, unlike classical bits, hold the potential for superposition and entanglement.[1] This is not just abstract; it's the source of quantum advantage.
- Classical Registers – The Bridge to Classical Understanding:
  - ○ Classical registers are our way of translating the ephemeral quantum world into the concrete classical realm.
  - ○ Practical Example: After applying a Hadamard gate to our coin qubit, we need to measure

it. The measurement result (0 or 1) is stored in the classical register.

○ Python

```
circuit.h(qr[0])  # Apply Hadamard gate
circuit.measure(qr[0], cr[0])   # Measure
and store the result
```

○

○

○ Educational Insight: Explain that measurement is a destructive process in quantum mechanics. The superposition collapses, and we get a classical outcome.

• Building Complex Circuits with Multiple Registers:

- Practical Example: Consider a scenario where you're implementing a simple quantum teleportation protocol. You'd need multiple qubits and classical bits.
- Python

```
qr_alice = QuantumRegister(1, 'alice')
qr_bob = QuantumRegister(1, 'bob')
qr_entangled = QuantumRegister(1, 'entangled')
cr_alice = ClassicalRegister(2, 'alice_meas')
cr_bob = ClassicalRegister(1, 'bob_meas')
circuit = QuantumCircuit(qr_alice, qr_bob, qr_entangled, cr_alice, cr_bob)
```

-
-

- Educational Insight: This demonstrates how Qiskit allows you to model complex quantum systems with multiple interacting components.

5.2 Creating and Manipulating Quantum Gates: The Quantum Operations (Advanced Techniques)

- Beyond the Basics: Unitary Gates and Customization:
  - Qiskit's unitary() method allows you to apply any arbitrary unitary matrix as a gate. This is incredibly powerful for implementing complex quantum operations.
  - Practical Example: Creating a custom phase shift gate.
  - Python

```
import numpy as np
from qiskit.extensions import UnitaryGate

theta = np.pi / 4
phase_gate = np.array([[1, 0], [0, np.exp(1j
* theta)]])
custom_gate  =  UnitaryGate(phase_gate,
label='Phase')
circuit.append(custom_gate, [qr[0]])
```

- o
- o
- o Educational Insight: This empowers you to go beyond standard gates and explore the full potential of quantum operations.
- Gate Decomposition: Bridging the Gap to Hardware:
  - o Real quantum hardware has limitations on the types of gates it can implement directly. Qiskit's gate decomposition tools

help you translate your circuits into hardware-compatible operations.[2]

- ○ Practical Example: Decomposing a Toffoli gate into CNOT and single qubit gates.[3]
- ○ Python

```
from qiskit.extensions import ToffoliGate
from qiskit.quantum_info import decompose_to_basis

toffoli = ToffoliGate()
decomposed_circuit = decompose_to_basis(toffoli)
```

- ○
- ○
- ○ Educational Insight: This illustrates the importance of

hardware awareness in quantum programming.
- Controlled Operations: Entanglement's Power:
  - Practical Example: Creating a Bell state.
  - Python

```
circuit.h(qr_entangled[0])
circuit.cx(qr_entangled[0], qr_bob[0])
```

  -
  -
  - Educational Insight: Emphasize how controlled operations are essential for creating entanglement, a key resource for quantum algorithms.
- Visualizing and Understanding Circuits:

- Practical Example: Using matplotlib to display the circuit.
- Python

```
import matplotlib.pyplot as plt
circuit.draw(output='mpl',
style={'backgroundcolor': '#EEEEEE'})
plt.show()
```

-
-
- Educational Insight: Visualization is crucial for debugging and understanding the flow of quantum information.

By focusing on practical applications and deeper educational insights, we can truly appreciate the power and versatility of Qiskit for building and simulating quantum circuits.

5.3 Building Quantum Circuits with Qiskit's Composer: A Visual Approach

Qiskit's Composer provides a graphical user interface (GUI) for constructing quantum circuits, making it an excellent tool for beginners and a valuable aid for visualizing complex circuits.[1]

- **Introduction to the Composer Interface:**
    - The Composer interface is accessible through the IBM Quantum Experience platform.
    - It offers a drag-and-drop interface for placing qubits, classical bits, and quantum gates.[2]

- The interface visually represents the flow of quantum information through the circuit.
- It's designed to be intuitive, allowing users to quickly create and modify quantum circuits.

- **Drag-and-Drop Functionality:**
  - Users can select quantum gates from a palette and drag them onto the circuit diagram.[3]
  - Qubits and classical bits can be added and positioned as needed.
  - Connections between gates and qubits are easily established.
  - This visual approach simplifies the process of circuit design, particularly for complex circuits.

- **Circuit Editing and Modification:**
  - The Composer allows for easy editing and modification of existing circuits.
  - Gates can be moved, deleted, or replaced.

- Circuit parameters, such as rotation angles, can be adjusted directly in the interface.[4]
- This flexibility enables users to experiment with different circuit configurations and optimize their designs.

- **Saving and Sharing Circuits:**
  - Circuits created in the Composer can be saved and shared with others.
  - Circuits can be exported in various formats, including QASM (Quantum Assembly Language) and Qiskit Python code.
  - This feature promotes collaboration and facilitates the sharing of quantum circuit designs.

- **Educational Benefits:**
  - The Composer provides a visual representation of quantum circuits, enhancing

understanding of circuit structure and operation.[5]

- o It simplifies the process of circuit design, making it accessible to beginners.
- o It allows for rapid prototyping and experimentation with different circuit configurations.
- o It is an excellent tool for teaching and learning quantum computing concepts.

5.4 Simulating Quantum Circuits with Qiskit's Simulators: Bringing Quantum Algorithms to Life

Qiskit's simulators allow you to execute quantum circuits on classical computers, providing a valuable tool for testing and debugging quantum algorithms.[6]

- **Qiskit Aer Simulators:**
  - Qiskit Aer provides a suite of high-performance simulators, including:
    - **State Vector Simulator:** Calculates the state vector of the quantum system after each gate application.
    - **Unitary Simulator:** Calculates the unitary matrix representing the entire quantum circuit.[7]
    - **QASM Simulator:** Simulates the execution of a quantum circuit as it would run on a real quantum device, including noise models.
    - **Stabilizer Simulator:** Efficiently simulates Clifford circuits.
  - These simulators offer different levels of fidelity and

performance, allowing you to choose the appropriate simulator for your needs.

- **Running Simulations:**
  - To run a simulation, you first need to create a QuantumCircuit object.
  - Then, you select the desired simulator backend using Aer.get_backend().
  - The execute() function is used to run the circuit on the selected backend.
  - The results are returned in a Result object, which contains information about the simulation, such as the statevector, counts, and unitary matrix.
- **Noise Simulation:**
  - Qiskit Aer allows you to simulate the effects of noise on quantum circuits.[8]

- Noise models can be created and applied to the simulators, providing a more realistic simulation of real quantum hardware.[9]
- This capability is essential for developing noise-resilient quantum algorithms.

- **Educational Value:**
  - Simulators provide a cost-effective and accessible way to test and debug quantum algorithms.
  - They allow you to explore the behavior of quantum circuits without requiring access to real quantum hardware.[10]
  - They enable the study of noise effects and the development of error mitigation techniques.

5.5 Visualizing Quantum Circuits and Results: Interpreting Quantum Information

Visualizing quantum circuits and simulation results is crucial for understanding and interpreting quantum information.

- **Circuit Visualization:**
    - Qiskit provides the draw() method to visualize quantum circuits.
    - The draw() method can output circuits in various formats, including text, LaTeX, and Matplotlib.
    - Visualizing circuits helps to understand the flow of quantum information and identify potential errors.
- **Result Visualization:**
    - Qiskit provides tools for visualizing simulation results,

such as histograms and statevector plots.[11]

- o Histograms are used to visualize the probability distribution of measurement outcomes.
- o State Vector plots visualize the complex amplitudes of the quantum state.[12]
- o Qiskit also integrates well with Matplotlib, allowing for custom visualizations.[13]

- **Bloch Sphere Visualization:**
  - o For single-qubit states, the Bloch sphere provides a powerful visualization tool.
  - o Qiskit provides functions for plotting qubits on the Bloch sphere, allowing you to visualize their state.[14]
  - o This is very useful for understanding the effects of single qubit gates.

- **Educational Importance:**

- Visualization tools enhance understanding of quantum circuits and simulation results.
- They facilitate the interpretation of quantum information and the identification of patterns.
- They provide a valuable aid for teaching and learning quantum computing concepts.

By mastering these tools, you can effectively build, simulate, and visualize quantum circuits, bridging the gap between theoretical quantum concepts and practical quantum programming.

CHAPTER 6

Cirq: Advanced Quantum Circuit Design

Cirq isn't just a quantum computing framework; it's a platform for exploring the frontiers of quantum information processing. Its architecture and design philosophy are tailored to support advanced research and development, particularly in the realm of near-term quantum devices.

6.1 Cirq's Architecture and Design Philosophy: A Framework for Exploration and Hardware-Aware Programming (Practical Focus)

- **Embracing Hardware Constraints: The "Device" Abstraction:**
  - Cirq's "Device" abstraction is a cornerstone of its hardware-aware design. Instead of assuming ideal qubits, Cirq encourages developers to model the specific limitations of their target quantum hardware.[1]
  - **Practical Example:** Imagine you're working with a superconducting qubit architecture. You can define a "Device" object that represents the connectivity constraints of the qubits, the available gate set, and the expected noise characteristics.[2] This allows you to compile your circuits in a way that minimizes errors and maximizes performance on that specific hardware.

- o **Educational Insight:** This emphasis on hardware awareness is crucial for bridging the gap between theoretical quantum algorithms and practical implementations. It fosters a deeper understanding of the challenges and opportunities presented by real quantum devices.
- **Parameterized Circuits and Variational Algorithms: A Playground for Optimization:**
  - o Cirq excels at handling parameterized quantum circuits, which are essential for variational quantum algorithms.[3] These algorithms, like the Variational Quantum Eigensolver (VQE) and the Quantum Approximate Optimization Algorithm (QAOA), are at the forefront of

near-term quantum computing research.[4]

- ○ **Practical Example:** You can create a parameterized circuit with adjustable rotation angles and then use a classical optimizer to find the optimal parameters that minimize a cost function. This approach is widely used in quantum chemistry and materials science for finding ground-state energies of molecules.[5]
- ○ **Educational Insight:** This demonstrates how Cirq facilitates the development of hybrid quantum-classical algorithms, which are expected to play a crucial role in the NISQ era.
- **Noise Modeling: Simulating Reality:**
  - ○ Cirq's robust noise modeling capabilities allow researchers to

simulate the effects of various noise sources on quantum computations.[6]

- Practical Example: You can model depolarizing noise, relaxation noise, and crosstalk noise, and then apply these noise models to your quantum circuits.[7] This allows you to assess the robustness of your algorithms and develop error mitigation techniques.

- Educational Insight: Understanding and mitigating noise is essential for building fault-tolerant quantum computers.[8] Cirq's noise modeling tools provide a valuable platform for exploring these challenges.

- **Open Architecture:**
  - Cirq's open architecture allows for the creation of custom gates and devices.[9] This is very

important for researchers who are trying to create new quantum gates, or simulate new potential quantum hardware.

6.2 Defining Qubits and Gates in Cirq: Building Blocks for Complex Quantum Programs (Advanced Techniques)

- **GridQubits: Modeling Physical Layouts:**
  - ○ Cirq's GridQubit class provides a natural way to represent qubits arranged in a two-dimensional grid, which is common in superconducting qubit architectures.
  - ○ **Practical Example:** You can create a grid of qubits that reflects the physical layout of your target quantum chip, and

then use this grid to define your quantum circuits. This makes it easier to visualize and manage qubit connectivity.

- ○ **Educational Insight:** This highlights the importance of considering the physical layout of qubits when designing quantum circuits.

- **Custom Gates: Extending Cirq's Functionality:**
  - ○ Cirq makes it easy to define custom quantum gates, which is essential for exploring new quantum operations.[10]
  - ○ **Practical Example:** You can create a custom gate that implements a specific quantum operation that is not included in Cirq's standard library.[11] This allows you to experiment with new quantum algorithms and protocols.

- ○ **Educational Insight:** This empowers you to go beyond standard gate sets and explore the full potential of quantum operations.
- **Parameterized Gates: Enabling Variational Algorithms:**
  - ○ Cirq's support for parameterized gates makes it easy to implement variational quantum algorithms.[12]
  - ○ **Practical Example:** You can create a parameterized rotation gate and then use a classical optimizer to find the optimal rotation angle that minimizes a cost function. This approach is widely used in quantum machine learning and quantum optimization.
  - ○ **Educational Insight:** This demonstrates how Cirq facilitates the development of hybrid quantum-classical

algorithms, which are expected to play a crucial role in the NISQ era.

- **Moments and Schedules: Precise Timing Control:**
  - Cirq's "Moment" and "Schedule" abstractions provide precise control over the timing of quantum operations.[13]
  - **Practical Example:** You can use moments to group quantum operations that are executed simultaneously, and then use schedules to define the timing of these moments. This is crucial for optimizing the performance of quantum circuits on real quantum hardware.
  - **Educational Insight:** This highlights the importance of timing control in quantum computing, especially in the presence of noise and decoherence.

By focusing on these practical examples and advanced techniques, you can gain a deeper appreciation for Cirq's capabilities and its role in advancing the field of quantum computing.

6.3   Constructing   Complex Quantum Circuits: Orchestrating Quantum Operations

Building complex quantum circuits in Cirq involves orchestrating a sequence of quantum operations, managing qubit interactions, and optimizing for hardware constraints.

- **Layered Circuit Construction:**
    - Cirq's Circuit object allows for the construction of quantum circuits layer by layer, using cirq.Moment objects. This approach provides fine-grained control over the timing of quantum operations.

- ○ **Practical Example:** You can create a circuit with multiple layers, where each layer represents a set of quantum operations that are executed simultaneously. This is particularly useful for optimizing circuits for specific hardware architectures.
- ○ **Educational Insight:** This layered construction allows for the creation of circuits that closely resemble the physical implementation of quantum algorithms, taking into account the limitations of real quantum devices.
- **Conditional Operations and Control Flow:**
  - ○ Cirq supports conditional operations, allowing you to execute quantum gates based on the outcome of classical measurements.[2]

- **Practical Example:** You can create a circuit that applies a specific quantum gate only if a classical measurement yields a certain result.[3] This allows you to implement quantum error correction protocols and other complex control flow mechanisms.
- **Educational Insight:** This demonstrates how Cirq enables the implementation of quantum algorithms that incorporate classical control, which is essential for many practical applications.
- **Subcircuits and Reusable Components:**
  - Cirq allows you to define subcircuits, which are reusable components that can be incorporated into larger circuits.
  - **Practical Example:** You can create a subcircuit that

implements a specific quantum operation, such as a quantum Fourier transform or a quantum adder, and then reuse this subcircuit in multiple parts of your circuit.

- ○ **Educational Insight:** This modular approach to circuit design promotes code reuse and simplifies the development of complex quantum algorithms.[4]

- **Gate Fusion and Optimization:**
  - ○ Cirq provides tools for optimizing quantum circuits, such as gate fusion and gate cancellation.[5]
  - ○ **Practical Example:** You can use Cirq's optimizers to combine adjacent single-qubit gates into a single gate, or to cancel out pairs of inverse gates. This can reduce the number of gates in your circuit and improve its

performance on real quantum hardware.

- ○ **Educational Insight:** This highlights the importance of circuit optimization for mitigating noise and improving the efficiency of quantum computations.

6.4 Simulating Circuits and Analyzing Results with Cirq: Bringing Quantum Programs to Life

Cirq's simulators provide a powerful platform for executing quantum circuits and analyzing the results.[6]

- **Cirq's Simulator Backends:**
  - ○ Cirq provides a high-performance simulator that supports various simulation

methods, including statevector simulation and density matrix simulation.[7]

- **Practical Example:** You can use Cirq's simulator to calculate the statevector of your quantum circuit after each gate application, or to simulate the effects of noise on your circuit using density matrix simulation.[8]

- **Educational Insight:** These simulators allow you to explore the behavior of quantum circuits in detail, providing valuable insights into the performance of your algorithms.[9]

- **Analyzing Simulation Results:**
  - Cirq provides tools for analyzing simulation results, such as histograms and statevector visualizations.
  - **Practical Example:** You can use Cirq's plotting functions to

visualize the probability distribution of measurement outcomes, or to plot the statevector of your quantum circuit on the Bloch sphere.

- ○ **Educational Insight:** These visualization tools help you to interpret the results of your simulations and to identify potential errors in your circuits.
- **Noise Simulation and Error Analysis:**
  - ○ Cirq supports detailed noise modeling, allowing you to simulate the effects of various noise sources on quantum computations.[10]
  - ○ **Practical Example:** You can create a noise model that represents the noise characteristics of your target quantum hardware, and then apply this noise model to your simulations.[11] This allows you to

assess the robustness of your algorithms and to develop error mitigation techniques.

- ○ **Educational Insight:** Understanding and mitigating noise is essential for building fault-tolerant quantum computers.[12] Cirq's noise simulation tools provide a valuable platform for exploring these challenges.

6.5 Working with Parameterized Circuits in Cirq: Enabling Variational Algorithms

Parameterized circuits are essential for variational quantum algorithms, which are at the forefront of near-term quantum computing research.[13]

- • **Defining Parameterized Gates:**

- Cirq allows you to define parameterized gates, which are gates whose parameters can be varied.[14]
- **Practical Example:** You can create a parameterized rotation gate, such as cirq.rz(theta), where theta is a parameter that can be adjusted.
- **Educational Insight:** This allows you to create families of gates with varying parameters, which is essential for optimization algorithms.

- **Creating Parameterized Circuits:**
  - You can create parameterized circuits by incorporating parameterized gates into your circuits.[15]
  - **Practical Example:** You can create a circuit that implements a variational quantum algorithm, such as VQE or

QAOA, by using parameterized gates to define the ansatz.[16]

- ○ **Educational Insight:** This demonstrates how Cirq facilitates the development of hybrid quantum-classical algorithms, which are expected to play a crucial role in the NISQ era.
- **Optimizing Parameters:**
  - ○ Cirq integrates seamlessly with classical optimization libraries, such as SciPy, allowing you to optimize the parameters of your circuits.
  - ○ **Practical Example:** You can use a classical optimizer to find the optimal parameters that minimize a cost function, such as the energy of a molecule or the solution to an optimization problem.
  - ○ **Educational Insight:** This highlights the importance of

classical optimization techniques in the context of variational quantum algorithms.

By mastering these techniques, you can leverage Cirq's advanced capabilities to design, simulate, and parameterize quantum circuits, opening up new possibilities for quantum computing research and development.

CHAPTER 7

Interoperability: Qiskit and Cirq Integration

The quantum computing landscape is evolving rapidly, with frameworks like Qiskit and Cirq offering unique strengths and capabilities. Interoperability between these frameworks is crucial for enabling researchers and developers to leverage the best of both worlds.

7.1 Converting Between Qiskit and Cirq Circuits: Bridging the Abstraction Gap

Converting circuits between Qiskit and Cirq involves translating the underlying quantum operations and data structures from one framework to another. This process allows you to leverage the specific features of each framework while working within a unified workflow.

- **Understanding the Differences:**
  - ○ **Abstraction Levels:** Qiskit and Cirq have different levels of abstraction.[1] Qiskit often operates at a higher level, while Cirq provides more fine-grained control over hardware interactions.
  - ○ **Gate Definitions:** While both frameworks support standard quantum gates, they may use different naming conventions or parameterizations.
  - ○ **Circuit Representation:** Qiskit uses QuantumCircuit objects, while Cirq uses Circuit objects, with different underlying data structures.
- **Conversion Techniques:**
  - ○ **Direct Translation (Where Possible):** For simple circuits

with standard gates, direct translation may be possible. This involves mapping Qiskit gates to their corresponding Cirq gates and vice versa.

- ○ **Intermediate Representation (e.g., QASM):** QASM (Quantum Assembly Language) can serve as an intermediate representation for converting circuits.[2] Both Qiskit and Cirq support exporting and importing circuits in QASM format.

  - ■ **Practical Example:**
    1. Export a Qiskit circuit to QASM.
    2. Import the QASM file into Cirq.
  - ■ **Educational Insight:** This demonstrates how QASM acts as a lingua franca for quantum circuits, facilitating

interoperability between different frameworks.

○

○ **Custom Conversion Functions:** For more complex circuits or custom gates, you may need to write custom conversion functions. These functions would map the specific operations and data structures of one framework to the other.

■ **Practical Example:** Creating a function that iterates through each gate in a Qiskit circuit, and then creates the equivalent Cirq gate, and places it into a Cirq circuit.

■ **Educational Insight:** This empowers you to handle complex circuit conversions and to extend the interoperability capabilities of these frameworks.

- **Challenges and Considerations:**
  - **Gate Decomposition:** Qiskit and Cirq may use different gate decomposition strategies. You may need to ensure that the decomposed gates are compatible between the frameworks.
  - **Noise Models:** Noise models are framework-specific. You may need to translate noise models or use framework-independent noise representations.
  - **Hardware Constraints:** Hardware constraints, such as qubit connectivity, may differ between the frameworks. You may need to adapt your circuits to the specific hardware constraints of each framework.

7.2 Using the Strengths of Both Frameworks: A Synergistic Approach

Qiskit and Cirq offer complementary strengths, making their integration a powerful approach to quantum computing development.

- **Qiskit's Strengths:**
  - **High-Level Abstractions:** Qiskit provides high-level abstractions for quantum programming, making it easier to develop and prototype quantum algorithms.[3]
  - **Extensive Libraries:** Qiskit offers a rich set of libraries for quantum algorithms, applications, and noise characterization.[4]
  - **IBM Quantum Experience Integration:** Qiskit seamlessly integrates with the IBM

Quantum Experience, providing access to real quantum hardware.[5]

- o **Large Community:** Qiskit has a very large and active community, which provides a great deal of resources and support.[6]
- **Cirq's Strengths:**
  - o **Hardware Awareness:** Cirq emphasizes hardware constraints, allowing for the development of circuits that are optimized for specific quantum devices.[7]
  - o **Noise Modeling:** Cirq provides robust tools for noise modeling, enabling the simulation of realistic noise effects.[8]
  - o **Parameterized Circuits:** Cirq excels at handling parameterized circuits, which are essential for

variational quantum algorithms.[9]

- o **Google Quantum Cloud Integration:** Cirq integrates well with Google Quantum Cloud, and provides access to Google's quantum hardware and simulators.[10]
- **Synergistic Applications:**
  - o **Algorithm Development and Prototyping (Qiskit):** Use Qiskit's high-level abstractions and extensive libraries to develop and prototype quantum algorithms.
  - o **Hardware-Aware Compilation (Cirq):** Convert Qiskit circuits to Cirq and use Cirq's hardware-aware compilers to optimize the circuits for specific quantum devices.
  - o **Noise Simulation and Error Mitigation (Cirq):** Use Cirq's

noise modeling tools to simulate the effects of noise and develop error mitigation techniques.[11]

- **Variational Quantum Algorithms (Cirq):** Use Cirq's parameterized circuits to implement and optimize variational quantum algorithms.[12]

- **Hardware Execution (Qiskit/Cirq):** Run the optimized circuits on real quantum hardware using the respective framework's integration with cloud platforms.[13]

- **Educational Importance:**
  - Interoperability promotes a deeper understanding of the strengths and limitations of different quantum computing frameworks.

- It encourages a collaborative approach to quantum computing development.
- It prepares you to leverage the best tools for the job, regardless of the framework.

By mastering the techniques of circuit conversion and leveraging the strengths of both Qiskit and Cirq, you can unlock new possibilities for quantum computing research and development.

7.3 Hybrid Quantum-Classical Algorithms Implementation: Blending Classical and Quantum Power

Hybrid quantum-classical algorithms are a cornerstone of near-term quantum computing. They leverage the strengths of both classical and quantum computing to tackle problems that are intractable for either alone.[1]

- **Understanding the Hybrid Approach:**
  - Hybrid algorithms divide a computational task into classical and quantum subroutines.[2]
  - The quantum component typically handles tasks that benefit from quantum speedup, such as simulating quantum systems or optimizing complex functions.[3]
  - The classical component handles tasks that are well-suited for classical computers, such as data processing, optimization, and control.[4]
  - The classical and quantum components interact iteratively, with the classical component feeding parameters or data to the quantum component, and

the quantum component returning results to the classical component.[5]

- **Key Components of Hybrid Algorithms:**
  - **Ansatz Design:** The quantum component typically involves a parameterized quantum circuit, known as an ansatz.[6] The ansatz defines the structure of the quantum computation and its parameters.[7]
  - **Cost Function:** A classical cost function is used to evaluate the performance of the quantum component.[8] The cost function is typically a function of the ansatz parameters.
  - **Classical Optimizer:** A classical optimization algorithm is used to find the optimal values of the ansatz parameters that minimize the cost function.[9]

- Quantum Measurement: The quantum component involves measuring the output of the ansatz to obtain classical data.[10]
- **Practical Implementation:**
  - **Variational Quantum Eigensolver (VQE):**
    1. VQE is a hybrid algorithm for finding the ground-state energy of a molecule or other quantum system.[11]
    2. The ansatz represents the wavefunction of the system, and the cost function is the expectation value of the Hamiltonian.
    3. A classical optimizer is used to find the ansatz parameters that minimize the energy.
    4. **Implementation Considerations:**

- Choosing an appropriate ansatz is crucial for the performance of VQE.
- The choice of classical optimizer can also significantly impact the convergence and accuracy of the algorithm.[12]

o **Quantum Approximate Optimization Algorithm (QAOA):**
  1. QAOA is a hybrid algorithm for solving combinatorial optimization problems.[13]
  2. The ansatz represents a sequence of quantum operations that approximate the solution to the problem.[14]

3. The cost function is related to the objective function of the optimization problem.

4. **Implementation Considerations:**
   - QAOA's performance depends on the choice of the ansatz and the number of layers in the circuit.[15]
   - Classical optimization techniques are used to find the optimal parameters for the ansatz.[16]

- **Workflow:**
  1. Define the problem.
  2. Design the ansatz.
  3. Define the cost function.
  4. Choose a classical optimizer.

5. Iteratively run the quantum circuit and update the parameters.
6. Analyze the results.

- **Educational Significance:**
  - Hybrid algorithms are essential for exploring the capabilities of near-term quantum devices.[17]
  - They provide a pathway to quantum advantage by combining the strengths of classical and quantum computing.[18]
  - They highlight the importance of interdisciplinary collaboration between quantum physicists and computer scientists.

7.4 Advanced Simulation Techniques Using Both Frameworks: Expanding Simulation Horizons

Advanced simulation techniques are essential for understanding the behavior of quantum systems and for developing robust quantum algorithms.[19] Qiskit and Cirq offer complementary simulation capabilities that can be leveraged to expand our simulation horizons.

- **Qiskit Aer's Advanced Simulation:**
    - **Noise Simulation:** Qiskit Aer allows for detailed noise simulation, including custom noise models and realistic noise parameters.[20]
    - **Stabilizer Simulation:** Aer's stabilizer simulator efficiently simulates Clifford circuits, which are a class of quantum circuits

that are widely used in quantum error correction.[21]

- **Extended Stabilizer Simulation:** Simulating non-Clifford gates within stabilizer circuits.
- **GPU Acceleration:** Aer supports GPU acceleration, significantly speeding up simulations of large quantum circuits.

- **Cirq's Hardware-Aware Simulation:**
  - **Device Simulation:** Cirq's device abstraction allows for the simulation of quantum circuits on specific hardware architectures, taking into account the limitations of real quantum devices.[22]
  - **Noise Models:** Cirq provides robust tools for defining and applying noise models, including

custom noise models and realistic noise parameters.[23]

- ○ **Density Matrix Simulation:** Cirq supports density matrix simulation, which is essential for simulating noisy quantum systems.[24]

- **Combining Frameworks for Enhanced Simulation:**
  - ○ **Hybrid Simulation:** Combine the strengths of Qiskit Aer and Cirq to perform hybrid simulations. For example, use Qiskit Aer for efficient simulation of Clifford circuits and Cirq for detailed noise simulation of non-Clifford gates.
  - ○ **Cross-Validation:** Use both frameworks to simulate the same quantum circuit and compare the results. This can help to validate the accuracy of the simulations and identify potential errors.

- ○ **Custom Simulators:** Leverage the extensibility of both frameworks to develop custom simulators tailored to specific simulation needs.
- **Simulation of Open Quantum Systems:**
  - ○ Both frameworks allow simulation of open quantum systems, that interact with the environment.
  - ○ This is very important for modeling real quantum hardware.
- **Educational Importance:**
  - ○ Advanced simulation techniques are essential for exploring the capabilities of quantum systems and for developing robust quantum algorithms.[25]
  - ○ They provide a platform for testing and debugging quantum algorithms before running them on real quantum hardware.[26]

- They enable the study of noise effects and the development of error mitigation techniques.[27]
- By understanding how to use both frameworks, a researcher is much more powerful.

By mastering the implementation of hybrid quantum-classical algorithms and exploring advanced simulation techniques, you can unlock new possibilities for quantum computing research and development.

Part III:

Quantum Applications and Advanced Topics

CHAPTER 8

Quantum Machine Learning with Qiskit and Cirq

Quantum Machine Learning (QML) is a rapidly evolving field that aims to leverage the power of quantum computing to enhance machine learning algorithms.[1] By harnessing the unique properties of quantum systems, such as superposition and entanglement, QML has the potential to tackle complex machine learning tasks that are intractable for classical computers.[2]

8.1 Introduction to Quantum Machine Learning: A New Frontier in AI

QML is not merely about replacing classical machine learning algorithms with quantum ones. It's about developing new algorithms and approaches that exploit the quantum advantage to solve problems more efficiently and effectively.

- **Motivation for Quantum Machine Learning:**
  - **Increased Computational Power:** Quantum computers have the potential to process vast amounts of data and perform complex computations much faster than classical computers.[3]
  - **Handling High-Dimensional Data:** Many machine learning problems involve high-dimensional data, which can be challenging for classical algorithms.[4] Quantum algorithms may provide more efficient ways to handle such data.[5]

- Exploring **Complex Patterns:** Quantum systems can exhibit complex patterns and correlations that may be difficult to capture with classical models.
- **Potential for Speedups:** Quantum algorithms may offer exponential or polynomial speedups for certain machine learning tasks.[6]
- **Key Concepts in Quantum Machine Learning:**
  - **Quantum Feature Maps:** Quantum feature maps are used to encode classical data into quantum states.[7] They map classical data points to high-dimensional Hilbert spaces, where quantum algorithms can operate.[8]
  - **Quantum Kernels:** Quantum kernels are used to measure the similarity between quantum

states.[9] They are analogous to classical kernels in Support Vector Machines (SVMs).

- o **Variational Quantum Algorithms:** Variational quantum algorithms are hybrid quantum-classical algorithms that are used to optimize the parameters of quantum circuits.[10] They are particularly well-suited for near-term quantum devices.
- o **Quantum Neural Networks:** Quantum neural networks are quantum analogues of classical neural networks. They use quantum gates and measurements to perform computations.
- o **Quantum Annealing:** Quantum annealing is a quantum optimization technique that can be used to solve certain machine learning problems.[11]

- **Challenges and Opportunities:**
  - **Noise and Decoherence:** Quantum computers are susceptible to noise and decoherence, which can affect the accuracy of QML algorithms.[12]
  - **Scalability:** Building large-scale, fault-tolerant quantum computers is a significant challenge.
  - **Algorithm Development:** Developing efficient and practical QML algorithms is an active area of research.
  - **Data Encoding:** Efficiently encoding classical data into quantum states is a crucial challenge.
  - **Applications:** QML has the potential to revolutionize various fields, including drug discovery, materials science,

finance, and artificial intelligence.[13]

- **Educational Importance:**
  - QML is a rapidly growing field with immense potential.[14]
  - Understanding QML is essential for preparing the next generation of data scientists and AI researchers.
  - QML requires a multidisciplinary approach, bringing together expertise from quantum physics, computer science, and mathematics.[15]

8.2 Quantum Support Vector Machines (QSVMs): Quantum-Enhanced Classification

Quantum Support Vector Machines (QSVMs) are quantum analogues of classical

Support Vector Machines (SVMs).[16] They leverage quantum kernels to perform classification tasks more efficiently than classical SVMs in certain scenarios.[17]

- **Classical Support Vector Machines (SVMs):**
  - SVMs are powerful classification algorithms that find a hyperplane that best separates data points belonging to different classes.[18]
  - SVMs use kernel functions to map data points to high-dimensional feature spaces, where they can be linearly separated.[19]
- **Quantum Support Vector Machines (QSVMs):**
  - QSVMs use quantum kernels to map data points to high-dimensional Hilbert spaces.[20]

- Quantum kernels can be computed more efficiently than classical kernels in certain cases, leading to potential speedups for classification tasks.[21]
- QSVMs can handle high-dimensional data more efficiently than classical SVMs.[22]

- **Key Concepts in QSVMs:**
  - **Quantum Feature Maps:** Quantum feature maps are used to encode classical data into quantum states.[23] They define the mapping from classical data points to quantum states.
  - **Quantum Kernels:** Quantum kernels are used to measure the similarity between quantum states.[24] They are defined as the inner product of quantum states.
  - **Kernel Matrix:** The kernel matrix is a matrix whose elements are the quantum

kernel values between pairs of data points.

- ○ **Optimization:** Classical optimization techniques are used to find the optimal hyperplane that separates the data points in the high-dimensional Hilbert space.

- **Implementation with Qiskit and Cirq:**
  - ○ **Qiskit Implementation:** Qiskit provides tools for implementing QSVMs, including quantum feature maps and quantum kernels.[25]
  - ○ **Cirq Implementation:** Cirq can be used to implement custom quantum feature maps and quantum kernels.
  - ○ **Hybrid Approach:** A hybrid approach can be used, where Qiskit is used for high-level tasks and Cirq is used for

implementing custom quantum operations.

- **Advantages of QSVMs:**
  - **Potential for Speedups:** QSVMs may offer speedups for classification tasks, particularly for high-dimensional data.[26]
  - **Handling Complex Patterns:** QSVMs can handle complex patterns and correlations that may be difficult to capture with classical SVMs.[27]
- **Challenges of QSVMs:**
  - **Noise and Decoherence:** QSVMs are susceptible to noise and decoherence, which can affect their accuracy.[28]
  - **Data Encoding:** Efficiently encoding classical data into quantum states is a crucial challenge.
  - **Kernel Design:** Designing effective quantum kernels is an active area of research.

- **Educational Importance:**
  - QSVMs are a promising application of QML.[29]
  - Understanding QSVMs requires knowledge of both quantum computing and machine learning.
  - QSVMs highlight the potential of QML to enhance classical machine learning algorithms.[30]

By exploring these concepts, you gain a deeper understanding of the potential and challenges of Quantum Machine Learning, and how Qiskit and Cirq can be used to implement powerful algorithms like QSVMs.

8.3 Variational Quantum Eigensolver (VQE) for Machine Learning: Optimization and Feature Extraction

The Variational Quantum Eigensolver (VQE) is a hybrid quantum-classical algorithm primarily used for finding the ground state energy of quantum systems.[1] However, its optimization capabilities make it a versatile tool for machine learning tasks.

- **VQE Fundamentals:**
  - **Variational Approach:** VQE uses a parameterized quantum circuit (ansatz) to approximate the ground state of a Hamiltonian.[2]
  - **Energy Minimization:** A classical optimizer adjusts the ansatz parameters to minimize the expectation value of the Hamiltonian, which corresponds to the ground state energy.[3]

- **Hybrid Nature:** VQE combines quantum computations (evaluating the Hamiltonian expectation) with classical optimization (adjusting ansatz parameters).[4]
- **VQE for Machine Learning:**
  - **Optimization Problems:** VQE can be adapted to solve optimization problems that arise in machine learning, such as finding optimal parameters for complex models.[5]
  - **Feature Extraction:** The ansatz in VQE can be viewed as a feature extractor, mapping input data to a high-dimensional quantum feature space. The optimized parameters of the ansatz can then be used as features for machine learning tasks.
  - **Kernel Methods:** VQE can be used to construct quantum

kernels, which can be used in kernel-based machine learning algorithms like Support Vector Machines (SVMs).

- o **Data Clustering:** VQE can be used to find optimal cluster assignments by encoding the clustering problem as a Hamiltonian.

- **Implementation Considerations:**
  - o **Ansatz Design:** Choosing an appropriate ansatz is crucial for the performance of VQE. The ansatz should be expressive enough to capture the relevant features of the data, but also efficient to implement on near-term quantum devices.
  - o **Classical Optimizer:** The choice of classical optimizer can significantly impact the convergence and accuracy of VQE.[6] Gradient-based optimizers are often used, but

they can be sensitive to local minima.[7]

- o **Hamiltonian Encoding:** Encoding the machine learning problem as a Hamiltonian is a key step in using VQE. The encoding should be efficient and preserve the relevant information.

- **Educational Importance:**
  - o VQE demonstrates the power of hybrid quantum-classical algorithms for machine learning.[8]
  - o It highlights the potential of quantum computing to solve optimization problems that are challenging for classical computers.
  - o It provides a framework for exploring new quantum feature extraction techniques.

8.4 Quantum Neural Networks (QNNs): Towards Quantum-Enhanced Deep Learning

Quantum Neural Networks (QNNs) are quantum analogues of classical neural networks.[9] They aim to leverage quantum computing to enhance the capabilities of deep learning models.

- **QNN Architectures:**
  - **Variational QNNs:** These QNNs use parameterized quantum circuits as layers, with classical optimizers adjusting the parameters.[10]
  - **Measurement-Based QNNs:** These QNNs use measurements to extract information from quantum states, which are then processed by classical neural networks.[11]

- ○ **Quantum Convolutional Neural Networks (QCNNs):** These QNNs apply quantum convolutional operations to quantum data, similar to classical CNNs.[12]
- ○ **Analog QNNs:** These QNNs use analog quantum systems, like photonic or superconducting devices, to perform computations.
- **QNN Advantages:**
  - ○ **Potential for Speedups:** QNNs may offer speedups for certain deep learning tasks, particularly for high-dimensional data.[13]
  - ○ **Handling Complex Patterns:** QNNs can capture complex patterns and correlations that may be difficult to model with classical neural networks.[14]

- Quantum **Feature Extraction:** QNNs can perform quantum feature extraction, mapping input data to high-dimensional quantum feature spaces.[15]
- **Implementation Challenges:**
  - **Noise and Decoherence:** QNNs are susceptible to noise and decoherence, which can affect their accuracy.[16]
  - **Scalability:** Building large-scale QNNs is a significant challenge.
  - **Training Algorithms:** Developing efficient training algorithms for QNNs is an active area of research.
- **Educational Importance:**
  - QNNs represent a promising direction for quantum-enhanced deep learning.[17]
  - They highlight the potential of quantum computing to

revolutionize artificial intelligence.
- They require a multidisciplinary approach, combining knowledge of quantum computing, deep learning, and optimization.

8.5 Data Encoding Techniques: Mapping Classical Data to Quantum States

Data encoding is a crucial step in QML, as it determines how classical data is represented in quantum states. Efficient and effective data encoding is essential for leveraging the quantum advantage.

- **Amplitude Encoding:**
  - **Concept:** Classical data is encoded into the amplitudes of a quantum state.[18]
  - **Advantages:** Efficient for encoding high-dimensional data.

- **Disadvantages:** Sensitive to noise and requires normalization.
- **Angle Encoding:**
  - **Concept:** Classical data is encoded into the rotation angles of quantum gates.
  - **Advantages:** Robust to noise and easy to implement.
  - **Disadvantages:** Requires more qubits to encode high-dimensional data.
- **Basis Encoding:**
  - **Concept:** Classical data is encoded into the basis states of qubits.
  - **Advantages:** Simple and easy to implement.
  - **Disadvantages:** Requires a large number of qubits to encode high-dimensional data.
- **Quantum Feature Maps:**
  - **Concept:** Classical data is mapped to high-dimensional

Hilbert spaces using quantum feature maps.

- ○ **Advantages:** Can capture complex patterns and correlations in the data.[19]
- ○ **Disadvantages:** Designing effective quantum feature maps is an active area of research.
- **Tensor Network Encoding:**
  - ○ **Concept:** Classical data is encoded into tensor networks, which are then mapped to quantum states.
  - ○ **Advantages:** Efficient for encoding structured data.
  - ○ **Disadvantages:** Complex to implement.
- **Implementation with Qiskit and Cirq:**
  - ○ **Qiskit:** Qiskit provides tools for implementing various data encoding techniques, including amplitude encoding, angle

encoding, and quantum feature maps.[20]

  - **Cirq:** Cirq can be used to implement custom data encoding schemes and quantum feature maps.
- **Educational Importance:**
  - Data encoding is a fundamental concept in QML.
  - Understanding data encoding techniques is essential for developing efficient and effective QML algorithms.
  - Data encoding highlights the importance of bridging the gap between classical and quantum data representations.[21]

By exploring these advanced techniques and applications, you'll gain a deeper understanding of the potential and challenges of Quantum Machine Learning, and how Qiskit and Cirq can be used to implement powerful algorithms.

CHAPTER 9

Quantum Optimization and Simulation

Quantum optimization and simulation are two of the most promising applications of quantum computing. They leverage the unique capabilities of quantum systems to solve complex problems that are intractable for classical computers.[1]

9.1 Quantum Approximate Optimization Algorithm (QAOA): Finding Near-Optimal Solutions

The Quantum Approximate Optimization Algorithm (QAOA) is a hybrid quantum-classical algorithm designed to find approximate solutions to combinatorial optimization problems.[2] It's particularly well-suited for near-term quantum devices.

- **Understanding Combinatorial Optimization:**
    - Combinatorial optimization problems involve finding the optimal solution from a finite set of possible solutions.[3]
    - These problems arise in various domains, including logistics, finance, scheduling, and artificial intelligence.[4]
    - Examples include the Traveling Salesman Problem, the Maximum Cut Problem, and the Minimum Vertex Cover Problem.[5]
- **QAOA Approach:**
    - QAOA uses a parameterized quantum circuit to approximate the solution to the optimization problem.[6]
    - The circuit consists of alternating layers of two types of operators: a problem

Hamiltonian and a mixing Hamiltonian.[7]

o The parameters of the circuit are optimized using a classical optimizer to minimize the expectation value of the problem Hamiltonian.[8]

- **QAOA Algorithm Steps:**
  o **Problem Encoding:** Encode the optimization problem as a problem Hamiltonian.
  o **Ansatz Construction:** Construct a parameterized quantum circuit (ansatz) consisting of alternating layers of the problem Hamiltonian and the mixing Hamiltonian.
  o **Parameter Optimization:** Use a classical optimizer to find the optimal parameters that minimize the expectation value of the problem Hamiltonian.[9]
  o **Measurement:** Measure the quantum state to obtain an

approximate solution to the optimization problem.[10]

- **Key Features of QAOA:**
  - **Hybrid Algorithm:** QAOA combines quantum computations with classical optimization.[11]
  - **Parameterized Circuit:** The circuit's parameters are optimized using a classical optimizer.[12]
  - **Approximate Solutions:** QAOA provides approximate solutions to optimization problems, which may be sufficient for many practical applications.[13]
  - **Near-Term Applicability:** QAOA is well-suited for near-term quantum devices.[14]
- **Implementation Considerations:**
  - **Problem Hamiltonian:** Encoding the optimization problem as a Hamiltonian is a

crucial step. The encoding should be efficient and preserve the relevant information.

- ○ **Mixing Hamiltonian:** The choice of mixing Hamiltonian can significantly impact the performance of QAOA.[15]
- ○ **Ansatz Depth:** The number of layers in the ansatz (depth) determines the expressiveness of the circuit and the quality of the approximate solution.
- ○ **Classical Optimizer:** The choice of classical optimizer can impact the convergence and accuracy of the algorithm.[16]

- **Applications of QAOA:**
  - ○ **Logistics and Supply Chain Optimization:** Finding optimal routes for delivery trucks or optimizing resource allocation.[17]
  - ○ **Financial Portfolio Optimization:** Maximizing returns while minimizing risk.[18]

- **Traffic Flow Optimization:** Reducing congestion and improving transportation efficiency.
- **Machine Learning:** Solving optimization problems that arise in machine learning, such as finding optimal parameters for complex models.[19]

- **Educational Importance:**
  - QAOA demonstrates the power of hybrid quantum-classical algorithms for optimization.[20]
  - It highlights the potential of quantum computing to solve real-world problems.
  - It provides a framework for exploring new quantum optimization techniques.

9.2 Quantum Simulation of Physical Systems: Unraveling the Mysteries of the Quantum World

Quantum simulation is a powerful application of quantum computing that aims to simulate the behavior of quantum systems.[21] It has the potential to revolutionize various fields, including materials science, chemistry, and physics.

- **Motivation for Quantum Simulation:**
  - **Classical Limitations:** Simulating complex quantum systems is computationally expensive for classical computers.[22] The number of variables required to accurately model these systems grows exponentially with their size.
  - **Quantum Advantage:** Quantum computers can efficiently simulate quantum

systems, providing a significant advantage over classical computers.

- ○ **Understanding Nature:** Quantum simulation allows us to study and understand the behavior of quantum systems that are difficult or impossible to study experimentally.[23]
- **Quantum Simulation Approaches:**
  - ○ **Digital Quantum Simulation:** Digital quantum simulation involves discretizing the time evolution of a quantum system and implementing it using a sequence of quantum gates.
  - ○ **Analog Quantum Simulation:** Analog quantum simulation involves building a physical system that mimics the behavior of the target quantum system.[24]

- **Key Concepts in Quantum Simulation:**
  - **Hamiltonian:** The Hamiltonian describes the energy of a quantum system.[25]
  - **Time Evolution:** The time evolution of a quantum system is governed by the Schrödinger equation.[26]
  - **Discretization:** Digital quantum simulation involves discretizing the time evolution into small steps.[27]
  - **Trotterization:** Trotterization is a technique for approximating the time evolution of a quantum system.[28]
- **Applications of Quantum Simulation:**
  - **Materials Science:** Simulating the properties of new materials, such as superconductors and topological insulators.[29]

- **Chemistry:** Simulating chemical reactions and molecular properties, such as protein folding and drug design.[30]
- **Physics:** Simulating quantum field theories, condensed matter physics, and high-energy physics.[31]

- **Implementation Considerations:**
  - **Hamiltonian Simulation:** Efficiently simulating the Hamiltonian of a quantum system is a crucial step.
  - **Error Mitigation:** Quantum simulations are susceptible to noise and errors, which can affect their accuracy.[32]
  - **Scalability:** Simulating large quantum systems requires a large number of qubits.

- **Educational Importance:**
  - Quantum simulation is a powerful tool for studying and

understanding quantum systems.[33]

- ○ It has the potential to revolutionize various fields, including materials science, chemistry, and physics.
- ○ It highlights the importance of interdisciplinary collaboration between quantum physicists and computer scientists.

By delving into these concepts, you'll gain a deeper understanding of the potential of Quantum Optimization and Simulation to solve real-world problems and advance scientific discovery.

9.3 Applications in Materials Science and Chemistry: Revolutionizing Molecular and Material Design

Quantum computing has the potential to transform Materials Science and Chemistry by enabling the simulation of complex quantum systems that are intractable for classical computers.[1]

- **Materials Science Applications:**
  - **Predicting Material Properties:** Quantum simulations can accurately predict the properties of new materials, such as their electronic structure, conductivity, and mechanical strength.[2]
  - **Designing Novel Materials:** Quantum computers can aid in the design of novel materials with specific properties, such as

high-temperature superconductors, topological insulators, and advanced catalysts.[3]

- **Simulating Material Defects:** Quantum simulations can model the behavior of defects in materials, which can significantly impact their properties.[4]
- **Understanding Material Behavior Under Extreme Conditions:** Quantum simulations can model material behavior under extreme conditions, such as high pressure and temperature.[5]
- **Battery Research:** Quantum Simulations can help design better battery materials, that have higher energy density, and are more stable.[6]
- **Nanomaterial Design:** Quantum simulation can help

design new nanomaterials for applications in electronics, medicine, and energy.[7]

- **Chemistry Applications:**
  - **Molecular Simulations:** Quantum computers can simulate the electronic structure of molecules, enabling the prediction of chemical properties and reaction pathways.[8]
  - **Drug Discovery:** Quantum simulations can aid in the design of new drugs by modeling protein-ligand interactions and predicting drug efficacy.[9]
  - **Catalysis:** Quantum simulations can model catalytic reactions, enabling the design of more efficient catalysts for chemical synthesis.[10]
  - **Understanding Chemical Reactions:** Quantum simulations can provide insights

into the mechanisms of chemical reactions, leading to a deeper understanding of chemical processes.[11]

- ○ **Quantum Chemistry Calculations:** Quantum computers can perform highly accurate quantum chemistry calculations, such as coupled cluster calculations, which are challenging for classical computers.[12]
- ○ **Development of new chemical sensors:** Quantum simulation can help create sensors that are more sensitive and accurate.
- **Implementation Considerations:**
  - ○ **Hamiltonian Construction:** Constructing accurate Hamiltonians for molecular and material systems is crucial.
  - ○ **Basis Set Selection:** Choosing appropriate basis sets for

electronic structure calculations is essential.

- ○ **Error Mitigation:** Quantum simulations are susceptible to noise and errors, requiring error mitigation techniques.[13]
- ○ **Computational Resources:** Simulating large molecular and material systems requires significant computational resources.[14]
- **Educational Importance:**
  - ○ Quantum simulations in Materials Science and Chemistry have the potential to accelerate scientific discovery and technological innovation.[15]
  - ○ They highlight the power of quantum computing to address real-world problems.
  - ○ They require a multidisciplinary approach, combining knowledge of quantum physics, chemistry, and materials science.

9.4 Solving Combinatorial Optimization Problems: Quantum-Enhanced Problem-Solving

Combinatorial optimization problems are ubiquitous in various domains, including logistics, finance, scheduling, and artificial intelligence.[16] Quantum computing offers the potential to solve these problems more efficiently than classical computers.[17]

- **Understanding Combinatorial Optimization Problems:**
  - Combinatorial optimization problems involve finding the optimal solution from a finite set of possible solutions.[18]
  - Examples include the Traveling Salesman Problem, the Maximum Cut Problem, the Minimum Vertex Cover Problem, and the Knapsack Problem.[19]

- **Quantum Approaches to Optimization:**
  - **Quantum Approximate Optimization Algorithm (QAOA):** QAOA is a hybrid quantum-classical algorithm that uses a parameterized quantum circuit to approximate the solution to optimization problems.[20]
  - **Quantum Annealing:** Quantum annealing is a quantum optimization technique that uses quantum fluctuations to find the minimum energy state of a system, which corresponds to the solution to the optimization problem.[21]
  - **Adiabatic Quantum Computing:** Adiabatic quantum computing involves gradually evolving a quantum system from a known initial state to the ground state of a

Hamiltonian that encodes the optimization problem.

- **Applications of Quantum Optimization:**
  - **Logistics and Supply Chain Optimization:** Finding optimal routes for delivery trucks, optimizing resource allocation, and scheduling deliveries.[22]
  - **Financial Portfolio Optimization:** Maximizing returns while minimizing risk.[23]
  - **Traffic Flow Optimization:** Reducing congestion and improving transportation efficiency.[24]
  - **Scheduling and Resource Allocation:** Optimizing scheduling for manufacturing, healthcare, and other industries.[25]
  - **Machine Learning:** Solving optimization problems that arise in machine learning, such as

finding optimal parameters for complex models.[26]

- **Cryptography:** Breaking certain cryptographic codes.
- **Implementation Considerations:**
  - **Problem Encoding:** Encoding the optimization problem as a Hamiltonian is a crucial step.
  - **Ansatz Design (QAOA):** Choosing an appropriate ansatz for QAOA is essential.
  - **Annealing Schedule (Quantum Annealing):** Designing an effective annealing schedule for quantum annealing is crucial.
  - **Error Mitigation:** Quantum optimization algorithms are susceptible to noise and errors, requiring error mitigation techniques.[27]
- **Educational Importance:**
  - Quantum optimization has the potential to revolutionize

various industries by providing efficient solutions to complex problems.[28]

- o It highlights the power of quantum computing to address real-world challenges.
- o It requires a deep understanding of optimization theory, quantum physics, and computer science.

By exploring these applications, you'll gain a deeper understanding of the practical impact of quantum computing in Materials Science, Chemistry, and Optimization, and how it's shaping the future of these fields.

CHAPTER 10

Quantum Error Correction and Fault Tolerance

Quantum Error Correction (QEC) and Fault Tolerance are indispensable for the realization of practical quantum computers.[1] Unlike classical computers, which are relatively robust to noise, quantum computers are extremely sensitive to environmental disturbances. This makes errors inevitable, necessitating sophisticated techniques to detect and correct them.

10.1 The Challenge of Quantum Noise: The Achilles' Heel of Quantum Computing

Quantum noise is the primary obstacle to building large-scale, fault-tolerant quantum computers.[2] It arises from various sources, including interactions with the environment, imperfections in quantum gates, and decoherence.[3]

- **Sources of Quantum Noise:**
  - **Decoherence:** Decoherence is the loss of quantum coherence due to interactions with the environment.[4] It causes qubits to lose their superposition and entanglement, leading to errors.[5]
  - **Gate Errors:** Imperfections in quantum gates can introduce errors during quantum computations.[6] These errors can be due to calibration errors, control errors, or noise in the control signals.
  - **Measurement Errors:** Errors can also occur during quantum measurements, such as misidentification of measurement outcomes.[7]

- ○ **Crosstalk:** Interactions between qubits can lead to crosstalk errors, where operations on one qubit unintentionally affect other qubits.[8]
- ○ **Thermal Noise:** Thermal fluctuations can introduce energy into the quantum system, leading to errors.
- **Impact of Quantum Noise:**
  - ○ **Reduced Fidelity:** Quantum noise reduces the fidelity of quantum computations, leading to inaccurate results.[9]
  - ○ **Limited Coherence Time:** Decoherence limits the coherence time of qubits, which is the time for which they can maintain their quantum states.[10]
  - ○ **Scalability Challenges:** Quantum noise poses a significant challenge to building large-scale quantum computers,

as errors accumulate with increasing qubit numbers and circuit depth.[11]

- **Characterizing Quantum Noise:**
  - **Quantum Process Tomography:** Quantum process tomography is a technique for characterizing the noise acting on a quantum system.[12]
  - **Randomized Benchmarking:** Randomized benchmarking is a technique for measuring the average error rate of quantum gates.[13]
  - **Noise Spectroscopy:** Noise spectroscopy is a technique for identifying the sources and characteristics of quantum noise.[14]
- **Educational Importance:**
  - Understanding quantum noise is essential for developing effective

error correction and fault tolerance techniques.

- o It highlights the importance of hardware development and noise characterization in quantum computing.
- o It emphasizes the need for a multidisciplinary approach, combining knowledge of quantum physics, computer science, and engineering.

10.2 Introduction to Quantum Error Correction Codes: Protecting Quantum Information

Quantum Error Correction (QEC) codes are designed to protect quantum information from noise.[15] They encode logical qubits into multiple physical qubits, allowing errors to be detected and corrected.[16]

- **Classical Error Correction vs. Quantum Error Correction:**
  - Classical error correction codes protect classical bits from errors by introducing redundancy.[17]
  - Quantum error correction codes protect qubits from errors by encoding them into entangled states.[18]
  - The no-cloning theorem prevents direct copying of qubits, making quantum error correction more challenging.[19]
- **Key Concepts in Quantum Error Correction:**
  - **Logical Qubits:** Logical qubits are encoded into multiple physical qubits to protect them from errors.[20]
  - **Encoding:** Encoding involves mapping logical qubits to entangled states of physical qubits.[21]

- Error **Detection:** Error detection involves measuring the parity of physical qubits to identify errors.
- Error **Correction:** Error correction involves applying corrective operations to physical qubits to restore the logical qubit state.
- **Syndrome Measurement:** The process of measuring the parity of physical qubits to identify errors.

- **Examples of Quantum Error Correction Codes:**
  - **Repetition Code:** The repetition code encodes a logical qubit into multiple physical qubits by repeating the logical qubit state.[22]
  - **Shor Code:** The Shor code encodes a logical qubit into nine physical qubits, providing

protection against bit-flip and phase-flip errors.[23]

- ○ **Steane Code:** The Steane code encodes a logical qubit into seven physical qubits, providing protection against single-qubit errors.[24]

- **Educational Importance:**
  - ○ Quantum error correction codes are essential for building fault-tolerant quantum computers.[25]
  - ○ They demonstrate the power of entanglement and redundancy in protecting quantum information.
  - ○ They require a deep understanding of quantum information theory and coding theory.

10.3 Surface Codes and Other Error Correction Techniques: Scaling Up Quantum Protection

Surface codes and other advanced error correction techniques are designed to scale up quantum error correction and achieve high fault tolerance.[26]

- **Surface Codes:**
    - Surface codes are a class of topological quantum error correction codes that are particularly promising for building large-scale quantum computers.[27]
    - They encode logical qubits into a two-dimensional lattice of physical qubits.
    - Errors are detected by measuring the parity of neighboring physical qubits.

- Surface codes are robust to local errors and have a high fault tolerance threshold.[28]
- **Other Error Correction Techniques:**
  - **Color Codes:** Color codes are another class of topological quantum error correction codes that offer similar advantages to surface codes.[29]
  - **Concatenated Codes:** Concatenated codes involve combining multiple layers of error correction codes to achieve higher fault tolerance.[30]
  - **Subspace Codes:** Subspace codes encode logical qubits into subspaces of the Hilbert space, providing protection against errors.
  - **Measurement-Based Error Correction:** Measurement-based error correction uses measurements

to detect and correct errors in quantum computations.[31]

- **Educational Importance:**
    - Surface codes and other advanced error correction techniques are crucial for building fault-tolerant quantum computers.[32]
    - They demonstrate the power of topological quantum error correction and concatenated coding.
    - They require a deep understanding of quantum information theory, coding theory, and topology.

10.4 Fault-Tolerant Quantum Computing: Achieving Reliable Quantum Operations

Fault-tolerant quantum computing involves designing quantum circuits and algorithms that can tolerate errors during quantum computations.[33]

- **Fault-Tolerant Gate Sets:**
    - Fault-tolerant gate sets are designed to minimize the propagation of errors during quantum computations.
    - They typically involve using transversal gates, which act independently on each physical qubit.[34]
- **Fault-Tolerant Measurement:**
    - Fault-tolerant measurement involves designing measurement protocols that can tolerate errors during measurement.
- **Fault-Tolerant Circuit Design:**
    - Fault-tolerant circuit design involves arranging quantum gates and measurements in a way that minimizes the propagation of errors.[35]
- **Threshold Theorem:**

- The threshold theorem states that if the error rate of physical operations is below a certain threshold, then arbitrarily long quantum computations can be performed with arbitrarily high fidelity.[36]
- **Educational Importance:**
  - Fault-tolerant quantum computing is essential for building practical quantum computers.[37]
  - It demonstrates the power of error correction and fault tolerance in achieving reliable quantum operations.
  - It requires a deep understanding of quantum information theory, coding theory, and computer science.

By exploring these concepts, you'll gain a deeper understanding of the challenges and techniques involved in building reliable quantum computers, and how quantum error correction and fault tolerance are paving the way for the future of quantum computing.

CHAPTER 11

Quantum Cryptography and Communication

Quantum cryptography and communication are revolutionizing the way we think about secure information transfer. By leveraging the fundamental principles of quantum mechanics, these technologies offer unprecedented levels of security and efficiency.[1]

11.1 Quantum Key Distribution (QKD): Secure Key Exchange Based on Physics

Quantum Key Distribution (QKD) is a revolutionary cryptographic protocol that enables two parties to establish a shared secret key with provable security based on the laws of quantum physics.[2]

- **Classical Cryptography Limitations:**
  - ○ Classical cryptographic methods, such as RSA, rely on the computational difficulty of mathematical problems.[3]
  - ○ These methods are vulnerable to advances in computing power, particularly the emergence of quantum computers.[4]
- **QKD Principles:**
  - ○ **Quantum Properties:** QKD leverages quantum properties, such as superposition and the no-cloning theorem, to ensure secure key exchange.[5]
  - ○ **Photon Polarization:** QKD protocols typically use photons to transmit quantum information, encoding bits in their polarization states.[6]
  - ○ **Eavesdropping Detection:** Any attempt to intercept or measure the photons will

inevitably disturb their quantum states, alerting the legitimate parties to the presence of an eavesdropper.[7]

- **QKD Protocols:**
  - **BB84 Protocol:** The BB84 protocol is one of the most widely used QKD protocols.[8] It involves encoding bits in different polarization bases and detecting errors based on discrepancies in the received polarization states.[9]
  - **E91 Protocol:** The E91 protocol utilizes entangled photons to establish a shared secret key.[10]
  - **B92 Protocol:** A simplified QKD protocol that uses only two non-orthogonal quantum states.[11]
- **QKD Steps:**
  - **Quantum Transmission:** Alice sends photons to Bob,

encoding bits in their polarization states.[12]

- o **Basis Reconciliation:** Alice and Bob publicly discuss the bases they used to encode and measure the photons.[13]
- o **Error Estimation:** Alice and Bob estimate the error rate based on the discrepancies in their measurement outcomes.
- o **Key Distillation:** If the error rate is below a certain threshold, Alice and Bob perform key distillation to extract a shared secret key.[14]
- **Advantages of QKD:**
  - o **Provable Security:** QKD offers provable security based on the laws of quantum physics.[15]
  - o **Eavesdropping Detection:** Any attempt to eavesdrop on the key exchange will be detected.[16]

- **Long-Term Security:** QKD keys are secure against future advances in computing power.[17]
- **Challenges of QKD:**
    - **Distance Limitations:** Photon transmission is limited by signal loss and noise over long distances.[18]
    - **Implementation Complexity:** QKD systems can be complex to implement and maintain.
    - **Cost:** QKD systems can be expensive compared to classical cryptographic methods.
- **Educational Importance:**
    - QKD is a groundbreaking application of quantum mechanics in cryptography.[19]
    - It demonstrates the power of quantum information theory in securing communication.
    - It requires a deep understanding of quantum physics,

cryptography, and communication.

11.2 Quantum Teleportation and Superdense Coding: Quantum Communication Protocols

Quantum teleportation and superdense coding are quantum communication protocols that leverage entanglement to transfer quantum information and classical information, respectively.[20]

- **Quantum Teleportation:**
  - **Concept:** Quantum teleportation allows the transfer of an unknown quantum state from one location to another without physically moving the qubit itself.[21]
  - **Entanglement:** Teleportation relies on the creation and sharing of an entangled pair of

qubits between the sender and the receiver.[22]

- ○ **Classical Communication:** Teleportation also requires classical communication to complete the transfer.[23]
- **Superdense Coding:**
  - ○ **Concept:** Superdense coding allows the transmission of two classical bits of information using only one qubit.[24]
  - ○ **Entanglement:** Superdense coding also relies on the sharing of an entangled pair of qubits.
  - ○ **Efficiency:** Superdense coding doubles the classical information capacity of a quantum channel.
- **Applications:**
  - ○ **Quantum Networks:** Teleportation and superdense coding are essential for building quantum networks.[25]
  - ○ **Quantum Communication:** They can be used to transmit

quantum information and classical information securely and efficiently.

- **Distributed Quantum Computing:** They can enable distributed quantum computing by transferring quantum information between quantum processors.

- **Educational Importance:**
  - Teleportation and superdense coding demonstrate the power of entanglement in quantum communication.[26]
  - They highlight the unique capabilities of quantum information processing.
  - They require a deep understanding of quantum information theory and entanglement.

11.3 Post-Quantum Cryptography and Security Implications: Preparing for the Quantum Threat

Post-Quantum Cryptography (PQC) is a field of cryptography that focuses on developing cryptographic algorithms that are resistant to attacks from both classical and quantum computers.[27]

- **Quantum Threat to Classical Cryptography:**
    - Shor's algorithm, a quantum algorithm, can efficiently factor large numbers, breaking widely used public-key encryption methods like RSA.[28]
    - This poses a significant threat to the security of current communication and data storage systems.
- **PQC Algorithms:**

- **Lattice-Based Cryptography:** Lattice-based cryptography relies on the computational difficulty of solving problems on lattices.[29]
- **Code-Based Cryptography:** Code-based cryptography relies on the computational difficulty of decoding random linear codes.[30]
- **Multivariate Cryptography:** Multivariate cryptography relies on the computational difficulty of solving systems of multivariate polynomial equations.[31]
- **Hash-Based Cryptography:** Hash-based cryptography relies on the security of cryptographic hash functions.[32]
- **Symmetric Key Quantum Resistant Algorithms:** Some symmetric algorithms are thought to be resistant to

quantum attacks, but key sizes may need to be increased.[33]

- **Security Implications:**
  - **Transition to PQC:** Organizations and governments need to transition to PQC algorithms to ensure the long-term security of their systems.[34]
  - **Standardization:** National Institute of Standards and Technology (NIST) is leading the effort to standardize PQC algorithms.[35]
  - **Key Management:** Secure key management is crucial for the effective implementation of PQC.
- **Educational Importance:**
  - PQC is essential for ensuring the security of communication and data storage in the quantum era.[36]

- It highlights the importance of proactive security measures in the face of technological advancements.
- It requires a deep understanding of cryptography, number theory, and computer science.

By exploring these concepts, you'll gain a deeper understanding of the transformative potential of Quantum Cryptography and Communication, and how they're shaping the future of secure information transfer.

CHAPTER 12

Advanced Qiskit and Cirq Features

Qiskit and Cirq are not just tools for basic quantum circuit design; they offer a wealth of advanced features that empower researchers and developers to explore the frontiers of quantum computing.[1]

12.1 Custom Gate Definitions and Extensions: Tailoring Quantum Operations

The ability to define custom gates is essential for implementing novel quantum algorithms and exploring new quantum operations.

- **Qiskit Custom Gates:**

- Gate **Class:** Qiskit provides the Gate class, which allows you to define custom gates by specifying their unitary matrices.
- QuantumCircuit.unitary(): You can also directly apply unitary matrices to qubits using the QuantumCircuit.unitary() method.
- **Control Extensions:** Qiskit allows you to create controlled versions of custom gates using the control() method, enabling multi-qubit operations.
- **Decomposition:** Custom gates can be decomposed into simpler gates using Qiskit's decomposition tools, making them compatible with specific quantum hardware.
- **Practical Example:** Creating a custom phase-shift gate with a variable angle.

○ Python

```
import numpy as np
from qiskit import QuantumCircuit
from qiskit.extensions import UnitaryGate

theta = np.pi / 3
phase_matrix = np.array([[1, 0], [0,
np.exp(1j * theta)]])
phase_gate = UnitaryGate(phase_matrix,
label='Phase')

qc = QuantumCircuit(1)
qc.append(phase_gate, [0]) #append the
custom gate to the circuit.
```

○

○

- **Cirq Custom Gates:**

- cirq.Gate **Class:** Cirq's cirq.Gate class allows you to define custom gates with fine-grained control over their behavior.
- cirq.MatrixGate: For gates defined by unitary matrices, cirq.MatrixGate provides a convenient way to create custom gates.
- **Parameterized Gates:** Cirq excels at handling parameterized gates, which are essential for variational quantum algorithms.[2]
- cirq.decompose(): Cirq offers tools for decomposing custom gates into simpler gates.
- **Practical Example:** Creating a parameterized rotation gate around an arbitrary axis.
- Python

```python
import cirq
import numpy as np

class ArbitraryRotationGate(cirq.Gate):
    def __init__(self, axis, angle):
        self.axis = axis
        self.angle = angle

    def _unitary_(self):
        # Calculate the unitary matrix based on
        axis and angle
        return np.cos(self.angle / 2) * np.eye(2)
-   1j    *    np.sin(self.angle    /    2)    *
np.array([[self.axis[2],  -self.axis[1]  +  1j  *
self.axis[0]],  [self.axis[1]  +  1j  *  self.axis[0],
-self.axis[2]]])

    def _num_qubits_(self):
        return 1

axis = (1, 1, 1) # Example axis
angle = np.pi / 4
rotation_gate = ArbitraryRotationGate(axis,
angle)
```

```
qubit = cirq.LineQubit(0)
circuit = cirq.Circuit(rotation_gate(qubit))
```

- o
- o

- **Educational Importance:**
  - o Custom gate definitions empower researchers to explore new quantum operations and algorithms.
  - o They allow for the implementation of specialized gates tailored to specific applications.
  - o They enhance the flexibility and extensibility of quantum programming frameworks.

12.2 Noise Models and Realistic Simulations: Bridging the Gap to Real Hardware

Accurate noise modeling is crucial for developing noise-resilient quantum algorithms and evaluating the performance of quantum hardware.[3]

- **Qiskit Noise Models:**
  - NoiseModel **Class:** Qiskit's NoiseModel class allows you to define custom noise models by specifying noise parameters for gates and measurements.
  - **Predefined Noise Models:** Qiskit provides predefined noise models for common noise sources, such as depolarizing noise and thermal relaxation.
  - **Noise Characterization:** Qiskit's noise characterization tools help you to measure and

characterize noise on real quantum devices.[4]

- o **Aer Noise Simulation:** Qiskit Aer simulators support noise simulation, allowing you to run quantum circuits with realistic noise models.[5]

- **Cirq Noise Models:**
  - o cirq.NoiseModel **Class:** Cirq's cirq.NoiseModel class allows you to define custom noise models with fine-grained control over noise parameters.
  - o **Channel Noise:** Cirq supports various types of channel noise, such as depolarizing noise, bit-flip noise, and phase-flip noise.[6]
  - o **Custom Noise Channels:** Cirq allows you to define custom noise channels, enabling the simulation of complex noise sources.[7]

- o **Density Matrix Simulation:** Cirq supports density matrix simulation, which is essential for simulating noisy quantum systems.[8]
- **Educational Importance:**
  - o Noise modeling helps to bridge the gap between ideal quantum computations and real-world implementations.[9]
  - o It enables the development of noise-resilient quantum algorithms and error mitigation techniques.
  - o It provides insights into the limitations and capabilities of near-term quantum devices.

12.3 Quantum Control and Pulse-Level Programming: Fine-Tuning Quantum Operations

Quantum control and pulse-level programming allow for precise control over the physical implementation of quantum operations.[10]

- **Qiskit Pulse:**
    - **Pulse Scheduling:** Qiskit Pulse allows you to create pulse schedules that define the timing and shape of control pulses.[11]
    - **Control Electronics:** Qiskit Pulse provides access to the control electronics of quantum hardware, enabling fine-grained control over qubit manipulation.[12]
    - **Calibration:** Qiskit Pulse is used for calibrating quantum gates and characterizing noise.[13]

- **Custom Pulses:** Qiskit Pulse allows to create custom pulses.[14]
- **Cirq Pulse:**
  - While Cirq is more focused on gate-level abstractions, it provides flexibility for integrating with pulse-level control systems.
  - Cirq's open architecture allows for the development of custom pulse-level control interfaces.
- **Educational Importance:**
  - Quantum control and pulse-level programming are essential for optimizing the performance of quantum hardware.[15]
  - They enable the development of high-fidelity quantum gates and error mitigation techniques.
  - They provide a deeper understanding of the physical implementation of quantum operations.

12.4 Cloud-Based Quantum Computing and Accessing Real Hardware: Bridging the Gap to Quantum Reality

Cloud-based quantum computing platforms provide access to real quantum hardware, enabling researchers and developers to run their quantum programs on physical devices.[16]

- **IBM Quantum Experience:**
  - Provides access to IBM's superconducting qubit quantum computers.[17]
  - Offers Qiskit Runtime for efficient execution of quantum programs.
  - Provides tools for calibrating and characterizing quantum hardware.[18]
- **Google Quantum Cloud:**

- Provides access to Google's superconducting qubit quantum computers and simulators.
- Offers Cirq for programming and controlling quantum hardware.
- Provides tools for noise characterization and error mitigation.[19]
- **Amazon Braket:**
  - Provides access to quantum hardware from multiple providers, including IonQ, Rigetti, and D-Wave.
  - Offers a unified interface for programming and running quantum programs.
- **Azure Quantum:**
  - Provides access to quantum hardware and software from multiple providers, including Honeywell and Quantum Circuits.
- **Educational Importance:**

- Cloud-based quantum computing platforms provide access to cutting-edge quantum technology.[20]
- They enable researchers and developers to test and validate their quantum algorithms on real hardware.
- They accelerate the development of quantum applications and the advancement of quantum computing.

By mastering these advanced features, you'll be well-equipped to explore the frontiers of quantum computing and contribute to the development of practical quantum applications.

CHAPTER 13

Building a Quantum Application from Start to Finish.

Creating a quantum application is a multi-faceted process that demands a blend of theoretical understanding, practical coding skills, and a systematic approach. Let's break down each stage of the development lifecycle, from defining the problem to running the application on real quantum hardware.

13.1 Defining the Problem: Laying the Foundation for Success

The first step in building any quantum application is to clearly define the problem you're trying to solve. This involves understanding the problem's scope, identifying its key parameters, and determining whether a quantum approach is indeed suitable.

- **Problem Identification:**
  - o **Real-World Relevance:** Identify a problem that has real-world relevance and potential impact.
  - o **Quantum Advantage Potential:** Determine if a quantum algorithm could provide a significant advantage over classical algorithms in solving the problem.
  - o **Problem Scope:** Define the scope of the problem, including its inputs, outputs, and constraints.
  - o **Clear Objectives:** Establish clear and measurable objectives for the application.
- **Problem Analysis:**

- ○ **Classical Approaches:** Analyze existing classical approaches to solving the problem, including their limitations and computational complexity.
- ○ **Problem Decomposition:** Decompose the problem into smaller, more manageable sub-problems.
- ○ **Quantum Suitability:** Assess the suitability of quantum algorithms for each sub-problem.
- ○ **Resource Requirements:** Estimate the quantum resources required to solve the problem, such as the number of qubits, gate depth, and runtime.[1]
- **Example Problem Definition:**
  - ○ **Problem:** Optimize the routing of delivery trucks in a large city to minimize delivery time and fuel consumption.

- **Quantum Approach:** Use QAOA to find near-optimal solutions to the routing problem.
- **Scope:** Optimize routes for a fleet of 10 trucks with 20 delivery locations.
- **Objectives:** Reduce delivery time by 20% and fuel consumption by 15%.

- **Educational Importance:**
  - A well-defined problem is crucial for the success of any quantum application.
  - It helps to focus development efforts and ensure that the application addresses a relevant problem.
  - It fosters a deeper understanding of the problem domain and the potential of quantum computing.

13.2 Algorithm Selection: Choosing the Right Quantum Tools

Once the problem is defined, the next step is to select an appropriate quantum algorithm or approach. This involves considering the problem's characteristics, the available quantum resources, and the desired level of accuracy.

- **Algorithm Evaluation:**
  - **Problem Suitability:** Evaluate the suitability of different quantum algorithms for the problem.
  - **Resource Requirements:** Consider the resource requirements of each algorithm, such as the number of qubits, gate depth, and runtime.
  - **Accuracy and Performance:** Assess the accuracy and performance of each algorithm,

including its potential for quantum speedup.

- ○ **Algorithm Complexity:** Understand the computational complexity of the selected algorithm.
- **Algorithm Implementation:**
  - ○ **Qiskit/Cirq Selection:** Choose a quantum programming framework (Qiskit or Cirq) based on the algorithm's requirements and the available hardware.
  - ○ **Algorithm Decomposition:** Decompose the algorithm into a sequence of quantum gates and measurements.
  - ○ **Circuit Design:** Design the quantum circuit that implements the algorithm.
  - ○ **Parameterization:** Parameterize the quantum circuit to allow for optimization.[2]
- **Example Algorithm Selection:**

- ○ **Algorithm:** Quantum Approximate Optimization Algorithm (QAOA).[3]
- ○ **Rationale:** QAOA is well-suited for combinatorial optimization problems like routing optimization.[4]
- ○ **Implementation:** Use Qiskit's QAOA implementation with a custom cost function and mixing Hamiltonian.[5]
- • **Educational Importance:**
  - ○ Algorithm selection is a critical step in building a quantum application.
  - ○ It requires a deep understanding of quantum algorithms and their capabilities.
  - ○ It highlights the importance of matching the algorithm to the problem.

13.3 Code Development: Translating Algorithms into Quantum Circuits

Code development involves translating the selected algorithm into a quantum circuit using a quantum programming framework.

- **Framework Selection (Qiskit/Cirq):**
    - Choose Qiskit for its high-level abstractions, extensive libraries, and integration with IBM Quantum hardware.[6]
    - Choose Cirq for its flexibility, hardware awareness, and noise modeling capabilities.[7]
- **Circuit Construction:**
    - Use the framework's API to construct the quantum circuit, including qubit allocation, gate application, and measurement operations.

- Implement the algorithm's logic using quantum gates and control flow structures.
- Parameterize the circuit to allow for optimization.

- **Classical Interface:**
  - Develop a classical interface to interact with the quantum circuit, including input data processing, parameter optimization, and result analysis.
  - Integrate with classical optimization libraries, such as SciPy, for parameter optimization.[8]

- **Code Optimization:**
  - Optimize the quantum circuit for performance, including gate decomposition, gate cancellation, and circuit compilation.[9]
  - Optimize the classical interface for efficiency, including data

processing and parameter optimization.

- **Example Code Development (Qiskit):**
- Python

```python
from qiskit import QuantumCircuit, Aer, execute
from qiskit.algorithms import QAOA
from qiskit.algorithms.optimizers import COBYLA
from qiskit.utils import QuantumInstance

# Define the problem Hamiltonian (cost function)
# ...

# Create the QAOA algorithm
qaoa = QAOA(optimizer=COBYLA(), quantum_instance=QuantumInstance(Aer.get_backend('qasm_simulator')))

# Run the algorithm
```

```
result                        =
qaoa.compute_minimum_eigenvalue(opera
tor=problem_hamiltonian)

# Analyze the result
# ...
```

-
-
- **Educational Importance:**
  - Code development is the practical implementation of quantum algorithms.
  - It requires proficiency in quantum programming and classical software development.[10]
  - It emphasizes the importance of code optimization and performance tuning.

13.4 Testing and Validation: Ensuring Accuracy and Reliability

Testing and validation are crucial for ensuring the accuracy and reliability of the quantum application.

- **Unit Testing:**
    - Test individual components of the quantum circuit and classical interface.
    - Verify that each component performs as expected.
- **Simulation Testing:**
    - Run the quantum circuit on a quantum simulator to verify its functionality and performance.[11]
    - Test the application with various input data and parameter settings.
    - Analyze the simulation results to identify potential errors or inconsistencies.

- **Noise Testing:**
  - Simulate the effects of noise on the quantum circuit and analyze its impact on the application's accuracy.
  - Implement error mitigation techniques to reduce the impact of noise.
- **Hardware Testing (If Available):**
  - Run the quantum application on real quantum hardware to evaluate its performance in a real-world environment.
  - Compare the hardware results with the simulation results.
- **Validation:**
  - Validate the application's results against known solutions or benchmarks.
  - Evaluate the application's performance against the defined objectives.
- **Educational Importance:**

- Testing and validation are essential for building reliable quantum applications.
- They require a systematic approach and attention to detail.
- They highlight the importance of error analysis and noise mitigation.

13.5 Hardware Execution: Bridging the Gap to Quantum Reality

Hardware execution involves running the quantum application on real quantum hardware.[12]

- **Cloud Platform Selection:**
  - Choose a cloud-based quantum computing platform, such as IBM Quantum Experience, Google Quantum Cloud, or Amazon Braket.[13]

- Consider the platform's hardware capabilities, pricing, and availability.
- **Hardware Access:**
  - Access the quantum hardware through the platform's API or SDK.
  - Submit the quantum circuit to the hardware for execution.
- **Result Retrieval:**
  - Retrieve the results from the hardware and analyze them.
  - Compare the hardware results with the simulation results.
- **Performance Evaluation:**
  - Evaluate the application's performance on the hardware, including accuracy, runtime, and noise effects.
- **Educational Importance:**
  - Hardware execution is the ultimate test of a quantum application.

- It provides valuable insights into the performance of real quantum hardware.
- It accelerates the development of practical quantum applications.

By following these steps, you can build a quantum application from start to finish, gaining valuable experience in quantum programming, algorithm development, and hardware execution.

CHAPTER 14

Quantum Computing and Artificial Intelligence: The future.

The convergence of Quantum Computing and Artificial Intelligence (AI) is poised to reshape the technological landscape, unlocking unprecedented capabilities and ushering in a new era of innovation.[1] This synergistic revolution promises to tackle some of humanity's most pressing challenges while also raising profound ethical and societal considerations.[2]

14.1 The Intersection of Both Technologies: A Powerful Alliance

The intersection of Quantum Computing and AI is not merely a confluence of two distinct fields; it's a symbiotic relationship where each enhances the other, creating a powerful alliance capable of tackling previously intractable problems.[3]

- **Quantum-Enhanced Machine Learning:**
    - **Speeding Up Training:** Quantum algorithms can accelerate the training process of machine learning models, particularly for complex datasets and high-dimensional feature spaces.[4]
    - **Improved Optimization:** Quantum optimization techniques, such as QAOA and VQE, can find optimal parameters for machine learning models more efficiently than classical methods.[5]
    - **Enhanced Feature Extraction:** Quantum feature maps can map classical data to

high-dimensional Hilbert spaces, enabling the extraction of more informative features for machine learning tasks.[6]

- **Quantum Kernels:** Quantum kernels can capture complex relationships between data points, leading to improved classification and clustering performance.[7]

- **AI-Driven Quantum Computing:**
  - **Algorithm Design:** AI can be used to automate the design of quantum algorithms, optimizing circuit parameters and gate sequences.[8]

  - **Noise Mitigation:** AI can develop sophisticated noise models to predict and mitigate errors in quantum computations.[9]

  - **Hardware Optimization:** AI can optimize the design and control of quantum hardware, improving qubit coherence and gate fidelity.[10]

- ○ **Quantum Error Correction:** AI can aid in the development and optimization of quantum error correction codes.[11]
- ○ **Quantum Control:** AI can be used to optimize pulse sequences for precise control of quantum systems.[12]
- **Synergistic Applications:**
  - ○ **Drug Discovery and Materials Science:** Quantum-enhanced AI can accelerate the discovery of new drugs and materials by simulating molecular interactions and predicting material properties.[13]
  - ○ **Financial Modeling:** Quantum-enhanced AI can improve financial modeling by performing complex simulations

and optimizing investment strategies.[14]

- ○ **Autonomous Systems:** Quantum-enhanced AI can enable the development of more intelligent and autonomous systems, such as self-driving cars and robotic systems.[15]
- ○ **Scientific Discovery:** Quantum-enhanced AI can accelerate scientific discovery by analyzing vast datasets and identifying complex patterns.[16]

14.2   Potential Future Applications: A Glimpse into the Quantum-AI Era

The future of Quantum Computing and AI holds immense potential for transformative applications across various domains.

- • **Personalized Medicine:**

- Quantum-enhanced AI can analyze individual genetic data and medical records to develop personalized treatment plans.[17]
- Quantum simulations can accelerate drug discovery and development, leading to more effective and targeted therapies.[18]

- **Climate Change Mitigation:**
  - Quantum-enhanced AI can optimize energy grids, develop new carbon capture technologies, and simulate climate change scenarios.[19]
  - Quantum simulations can aid in the design of new materials for solar panels and batteries.[20]

- **Advanced Manufacturing:**
  - Quantum-enhanced AI can optimize manufacturing processes, design new materials, and develop intelligent robotic systems.[21]

- Quantum simulations can aid in the design of new nanomaterials and advanced manufacturing techniques.[22]
- **Space Exploration:**
  - Quantum-enhanced AI can optimize spacecraft trajectories, analyze astronomical data, and develop intelligent robotic systems for space exploration.[23]
  - Quantum simulations can aid in the design of new materials for spacecraft and space habitats.[24]
- **Fundamental Science:**
  - Quantum-enhanced AI can accelerate scientific discovery by analyzing vast datasets and identifying complex patterns in physics, chemistry, and biology.[25]
  - Quantum simulations can aid in the study of fundamental physics, such as quantum

gravity and the nature of dark matter.[26]

- **Cybersecurity:**
  - Quantum-enhanced AI can develop more robust cryptographic algorithms and detect cyber threats more effectively.[27]
  - Quantum communication networks can provide secure communication channels.[28]
- **Financial Modeling and Prediction:**
  - Quantum AI can be used for more accurate financial modeling, fraud detection, and risk management.[29]

14.3 Ethical and Societal Impacts: Navigating the Quantum-AI Frontier Responsibly

The transformative potential of Quantum Computing and AI also raises profound ethical and societal considerations that must be addressed proactively.[30]

- **Job Displacement:**
    - Automation driven by Quantum-enhanced AI may lead to job displacement in certain industries.
    - It's crucial to invest in education and training programs to prepare the workforce for the changing job market.
- **Bias and Discrimination:**
    - Quantum-enhanced AI algorithms can inherit biases from the data they are trained

on, leading to discriminatory outcomes.[31]

  o It's essential to develop AI systems that are fair, transparent, and accountable.

- **Privacy Concerns:**
  o Quantum-enhanced AI can analyze vast amounts of personal data, raising privacy concerns.[32]
  o It's crucial to develop robust data privacy and security measures.

- **Autonomous Weapons:**
  o Quantum-enhanced AI could be used to develop autonomous weapons systems, raising ethical concerns about the use of lethal force.[33]
  o It's essential to establish international norms and regulations for the development and use of autonomous weapons.

- **Access and Equity:**
  - The benefits of Quantum-enhanced AI may not be distributed equitably, exacerbating existing social and economic inequalities.
  - It's crucial to ensure that everyone has access to the benefits of these technologies.
- **Misinformation and Manipulation:**
  - Quantum-enhanced AI could be used to create deepfakes and spread misinformation, undermining trust in information and institutions.
  - It's essential to develop robust mechanisms for detecting and countering misinformation.
- **Existential Risks:**
  - Some experts have raised concerns about the potential existential risks posed by advanced AI systems.

- It's crucial to engage in responsible AI research and development, and to develop safety measures to mitigate potential risks.

- **Educational Importance:**
    - It is crucial to have open and informed discussions about the ethical and societal implications of Quantum Computing and AI.
    - It is important to develop policies and regulations that promote responsible innovation and mitigate potential risks.
    - It is vital to ensure that the benefits of these technologies are shared equitably and that everyone has a voice in shaping their future.

By engaging in thoughtful discussions and proactive measures, we can harness the transformative power of Quantum

Computing and AI for the benefit of humanity while mitigating potential risks.

Part IV

Conclusion and Appendices

CHAPTER 15

Conclusion: The Quantum Computing Revolution

Our journey through the realm of quantum computing has revealed a field brimming with potential, poised to revolutionize industries, redefine scientific understanding, and reshape the very fabric of computation. As we approach the dawn of this quantum era, it's crucial to reflect on the key takeaways, envision the future, and understand the opportunities and challenges that lie ahead.

15.1 Summary of Key Concepts and Techniques: The Quantum Toolkit

Throughout our exploration, we've encountered a rich array of concepts and techniques that form the foundation of quantum computing. Let's summarize the essential components of the quantum toolkit:

- **Qubits and Superposition:** The fundamental unit of quantum information, capable of existing in multiple states simultaneously.[1]
- **Entanglement:** The phenomenon of interconnected quantum states, enabling correlations beyond classical possibilities.[2]
- **Quantum Gates:** The building blocks of quantum circuits, manipulating qubits to perform computations.[3]
- **Quantum Circuits:** Sequences of quantum gates and measurements that implement quantum algorithms.[4]
- **Tensor Products:** Mathematical tools for combining qubit states into multi-qubit systems.[5]

- **Quantum Fourier Transform (QFT):** A powerful algorithm for manipulating quantum states in the frequency domain.
- **Quantum Algorithms:** Algorithms like Grover's search and Shor's factoring, demonstrating quantum speedups for specific problems.[6]
- **Hybrid Quantum-Classical Algorithms:** Algorithms like VQE and QAOA, leveraging both quantum and classical resources.[7]
- **Quantum Error Correction (QEC):** Techniques for protecting quantum information from noise and decoherence.[8]
- **Quantum Key Distribution (QKD):** Protocols for secure key exchange based on quantum physics.[9]
- **Qiskit and Cirq:** Open-source frameworks for quantum programming, simulation, and hardware access.[10]

- **Quantum Machine Learning (QML):** Applying quantum computing to enhance machine learning algorithms.[11]
- **Quantum Simulation:** Using quantum computers to model and understand complex quantum systems.[12]
- **Noise Models and Realistic Simulations:** Tools for simulating the effects of noise on quantum computations.[13]
- **Quantum Control and Pulse-Level Programming:** Fine-tuning quantum operations at the physical level.

15.2 The Future of Quantum Computing and Its Impact: A Transformative Force

The future of quantum computing is bright, with the potential to transform numerous industries and scientific disciplines.[14]

- **Scientific Discovery:** Quantum simulations will accelerate discoveries in materials science, chemistry, and drug discovery.[15]
- **Artificial Intelligence:** Quantum-enhanced AI will lead to breakthroughs in machine learning, optimization, and data analysis.[16]
- **Cryptography:** Quantum-resistant cryptography will safeguard sensitive information in the quantum era.[17]
- **Finance:** Quantum algorithms will optimize financial portfolios, detect fraud, and improve risk management.[18]
- **Logistics and Optimization:** Quantum optimization will solve complex routing and scheduling problems.[19]
- **Healthcare:** Quantum computing will enable personalized medicine and accelerate drug development.[20]

- **Energy:** Quantum simulations will aid in the design of new energy materials and optimize energy grids.[21]
- **Communication:** Quantum communication networks will provide secure and efficient information transfer.[22]
- **Fundamental Physics:** Quantum computers will help us understand the universe at its most fundamental level.

15.3 Opportunities and Challenges in the Field: Navigating the Quantum Landscape

The quantum computing field presents both exciting opportunities and significant challenges.

- **Opportunities:**
  - **Algorithm Development:** Developing new quantum

algorithms for diverse applications.

- **Hardware Engineering:** Building scalable and fault-tolerant quantum computers.
- **Software Development:** Creating user-friendly quantum programming tools and platforms.
- **Application Development:** Exploring and developing quantum applications for various industries.
- **Research and Innovation:** Pushing the boundaries of quantum computing through research and development.
- **Education and Training:** Preparing the next generation of quantum computing experts.
- **Challenges:**

- **Noise and Decoherence:** Overcoming the limitations imposed by quantum noise.
- **Scalability:** Building large-scale quantum computers with a sufficient number of qubits.
- **Error Correction:** Developing robust and efficient quantum error correction techniques.[23]
- **Algorithm Efficiency:** Designing quantum algorithms that provide significant speedups over classical algorithms.[24]
- **Hardware Availability:** Increasing access to quantum hardware for research and development.
- **Talent Gap:** Addressing the shortage of skilled quantum computing professionals.[25]
- **Ethical and Societal Impacts:** Navigating the ethical

and societal implications of quantum technologies.

15.4 Next Steps for Learning Quantum Computing: Embarking on the Quantum Journey

For those eager to delve deeper into the world of quantum computing, here are some recommended next steps:

- **Online Courses and Tutorials:** Explore online courses and tutorials offered by universities and platforms like Coursera, edX, and Quantum Computing Report.
- **Textbooks and Research Papers:** Study foundational textbooks on quantum computing and explore cutting-edge research papers.
- **Open-Source Frameworks:** Experiment with Qiskit and Cirq to

gain hands-on experience in quantum programming.[26]

- **Quantum Computing Communities:** Join online communities and forums to connect with other quantum computing enthusiasts.
- **Hackathons and Competitions:** Participate in quantum computing hackathons and competitions to test your skills and learn from others.[27]
- **Research Projects:** Engage in research projects to contribute to the advancement of quantum computing.
- **Attend Conferences and Workshops:** Attend conferences and workshops to stay up-to-date on the latest developments in the field.
- **Build a strong foundation in Linear Algebra, and Quantum Mechanics:** these subjects are vital for success in the field.
- **Practice coding on real quantum hardware:** When possible, run code

on real quantum devices to see how they function in reality.

The quantum computing revolution is underway, and its impact will be felt across all aspects of society. By embracing the opportunities and addressing the challenges, we can shape a future where quantum computing empowers us to solve some of humanity's most pressing problems and unlock the mysteries of the universe.

Appendix A: Mathematical Foundations Review

The realm of quantum computing is built upon a solid bedrock of mathematical principles.[1] This appendix aims to reinforce and expand your understanding of complex numbers, matrix operations, eigenvalues, and probability distributions, providing the essential toolkit for your quantum journey.

A.1 Complex Numbers and Their Properties: Beyond the Real Line – A World of Phases and Amplitudes

Complex numbers are not just mathematical curiosities; they are the lifeblood of quantum mechanics. They provide a natural framework for describing the wave-like nature of quantum particles and the probabilistic outcomes of quantum measurements.[2]

- The Power of "i": Unveiling Hidden Dimensions
  - The imaginary unit "i" ($\sqrt{-1}$) introduces a dimension orthogonal to the real number line, allowing us to represent quantities that involve oscillations and rotations.
  - In quantum mechanics, "i" is crucial for describing the time evolution of quantum states, as seen in the Schrödinger equation.
- Visualizing Complex Numbers: The Argand Diagram
  - The Argand diagram (complex plane) provides a powerful visual representation of complex numbers.[3] The real part is plotted along the horizontal axis, and the imaginary part along the vertical axis.[4]
  - This visualization helps to understand complex number

operations geometrically.[5] For example, multiplication corresponds to rotation and scaling in the complex plane.

- Euler's Formula: The Bridge Between Exponentials and Trigonometry
  - Euler's formula ($e^{\wedge}(i\theta) = \cos \theta + i \sin \theta$) is a mathematical masterpiece that connects complex exponentials to trigonometric functions.[6]
  - This formula is fundamental in quantum mechanics, as it allows us to represent quantum states and operations using complex exponentials, which are often more convenient to work with.
- Complex Conjugate: Mirroring the Imaginary World
  - The complex conjugate of a complex number "z" is obtained by flipping the sign of its imaginary part (z^*).[7]

○ The complex conjugate is essential for calculating the magnitude of a complex number and for performing various operations in quantum mechanics.

- Applications in Quantum Computing: The Language of Quantum States

  ○ **Qubit Amplitudes:** The state of a qubit is described by a superposition of $|0\rangle$ and $|1\rangle$, with complex amplitudes determining the probability of measuring each state.[8]

  ○ **Phase Factors:** Complex phase factors play a crucial role in quantum interference, which is the basis of many quantum algorithms.[9]

  ○ **Unitary Evolution:** Quantum gates are represented by unitary matrices with complex entries, ensuring that quantum operations preserve the norm of quantum states.[10]

- Educational Importance:
  - Complex numbers provide the mathematical foundation for understanding quantum superposition, entanglement, and interference.[11]
  - They are essential for working with quantum states, quantum gates, and quantum algorithms.

A.2 Matrix Operations and Eigenvalues: The Algebra of Quantum Transformations

Matrices are the mathematical tools that describe quantum transformations, representing both quantum gates and observables.[12] Eigenvalues and eigenvectors provide insights into the fundamental properties of these transformations.

- Matrix Multiplication: Composing Quantum Operations
  - Matrix multiplication represents the composition of quantum operations. Applying one quantum gate followed by another is equivalent to multiplying their corresponding matrices.
  - Understanding matrix multiplication is crucial for analyzing the behavior of quantum circuits.
- Hermitian Matrices: The Observables of the Quantum World
  - Hermitian matrices represent physical observables in quantum mechanics.[13] Their eigenvalues correspond to the possible measurement outcomes, and their eigenvectors correspond to the associated quantum states.
  - The fact that Hermitian matrices have real eigenvalues ensures

that measurement outcomes are real numbers.[14]

- Unitary Matrices: Preserving Quantum Information
  - Unitary matrices represent quantum gates, which preserve the norm of quantum states.[15] This ensures that quantum operations do not change the overall probability of measurement outcomes.
  - Unitary transformations are reversible, meaning that any quantum gate can be undone by applying its inverse.[16]
- Eigenvalues and Eigenvectors: Unveiling Hidden Properties
  - Eigenvalues and eigenvectors provide insights into the fundamental properties of matrices.[17] Eigenvalues represent the scaling factors of eigenvectors under a linear transformation.[18]

- In quantum mechanics, eigenvalues and eigenvectors are used to determine the possible measurement outcomes and the corresponding quantum states of a system.[19]
- Applications in Quantum Computing: The Foundation of Quantum Algorithms
  - **Quantum Gate Representation:** Quantum gates are represented by unitary matrices, which act on qubit states represented as vectors.[20]
  - **Observable Measurement:** Measurement of observables is described by Hermitian matrices, with eigenvalues representing possible outcomes.
  - **Hamiltonian Evolution:** The time evolution of quantum systems is governed by the Schrödinger equation, which involves matrix exponentials.

- Educational Importance:
  - Matrix operations and eigenvalues provide the mathematical framework for understanding quantum transformations and measurements.[21]
  - They are essential for working with quantum gates, observables, and quantum algorithms.

A.3 Probability Distributions and Statistical Concepts: Quantifying Uncertainty in the Quantum Realm

Quantum mechanics is inherently probabilistic, meaning that measurement outcomes are not deterministic.[22] Probability distributions and statistical concepts provide the tools for quantifying and analyzing this uncertainty.[23]

- Probability Amplitudes and Distributions: The Language of Quantum Outcomes
  - In quantum mechanics, probability amplitudes are complex numbers whose squared magnitudes give the probabilities of measurement outcomes.[24]
  - Probability distributions describe the likelihood of different measurement outcomes, allowing us to quantify the uncertainty in quantum measurements.[25]
- Mean and Variance: Characterizing Quantum Data
  - The mean and variance are statistical measures that characterize the central tendency and spread of quantum data.[26]

- These measures are used to analyze the results of quantum experiments and to evaluate the performance of quantum algorithms.
- Statistical Independence: Understanding Correlations
  - Statistical independence describes the absence of correlations between random variables.[27] In quantum mechanics, entanglement leads to correlations that violate classical notions of independence.[28]
  - Understanding statistical independence is crucial for analyzing quantum data and for developing quantum communication protocols.
- Applications in Quantum Computing: Analyzing and Interpreting Quantum Data

- Measurement Statistics: Probability distributions are used to analyze the statistics of quantum measurement outcomes.[29]
- Error Analysis: Statistical concepts are used to quantify and analyze errors in quantum computations.[30]
- Quantum Sampling: Quantum algorithms can be used to sample from probability distributions, which has applications in quantum machine learning and simulation.[31]
- Educational Importance:
  - Probability distributions and statistical concepts are essential for understanding the probabilistic nature of quantum mechanics.
  - They provide the tools for analyzing quantum data,

evaluating the performance of quantum algorithms, and developing quantum error correction techniques.

By mastering these mathematical foundations, you will unlock a deeper understanding of the quantum world and be well-prepared to explore the exciting possibilities of quantum computing.

Appendix B: Qiskit and Cirq Installation and Troubleshooting

Setting up your quantum development environment is the first step toward exploring the exciting world of quantum computing. This appendix provides detailed installation instructions, troubleshooting tips, and a list of essential resources to ensure a smooth and productive experience with Qiskit and Cirq.

B.1 Detailed Installation Instructions for Different Operating Systems: Getting Started with Qiskit and Cirq

Qiskit and Cirq are Python-based frameworks, so you'll need Python and pip (Python's package installer) installed on your system.[1] We'll cover installation instructions for Windows, macOS, and Linux.

- **Prerequisites:**
  - **Python:** Ensure you have Python 3.7 or later installed.[2] You can download the latest version from python.org.
  - **pip:** pip is usually included with Python installations.[3] Verify its installation by running python

`-m pip --version` in your terminal.

- ○ **Virtual Environments (Recommended):** It's highly recommended to use virtual environments to isolate your project dependencies.[4] This prevents conflicts between different Python projects.[5]
  - To create a virtual environment, use `python -m venv myenv` (replace `myenv` with your desired environment name).
  - Activate the environment:
    - **Windows:** `myenv\Scripts\activate`
    - **macOS/Linux:** `source myenv/bin/activate`
  - ○
- **Qiskit Installation:**
  - ○ **Using pip:**

- Open your terminal or command prompt.
- Activate your virtual environment (if used).
- Run `pip install qiskit` to install the core Qiskit package.
- To install additional Qiskit components (e.g., Aer for simulators, Ignis for noise characterization, etc.), run:
  - `pip install qiskit-aer`
  - `pip install qiskit-ignis`
  - `pip install qiskit-ibmq-provider` (for IBM Quantum Experience access)
- Verify the installation by running `python -c "import qiskit; print(qiskit.__version__)"`
.

- **Cirq Installation:**
  - **Using pip:**
    - Open your terminal or command prompt.
    - Activate your virtual environment (if used).
    - Run `pip install cirq` to install the core Cirq package.
    - Verify the installation by running `python -c "import cirq; print(cirq.__version__)"`.
- **Operating System-Specific Notes:**
  - **Windows:**
    - Ensure that Python and pip are added to your system's PATH environment variable.
    - If you encounter issues with installing certain packages, consider

installing Microsoft Visual
C++ Build Tools.

- ○ **macOS:**
  - ■ Xcode Command Line
    Tools are often required
    for compiling certain
    packages. Install them by
    running `xcode-select
    --install` in your terminal.
  - ■ Consider using Homebrew
    to manage Python and
    other dependencies.
- ○ **Linux (Ubuntu/Debian):**
  - ■ Use `apt-get` or `apt` to
    install Python and pip:
    `sudo apt-get update &&
    sudo apt-get install
    python3 python3-pip`.
  - ■ Install build essentials:
    `sudo apt-get install
    build-essential`.
- ○ **Linux (Fedora/CentOS):**
  - ■ Use `dnf` or `yum` to install
    Python and pip: `sudo dnf`

install python3
python3-pip.
- Install development tools:
sudo dnf groupinstall
"Development Tools".

B.2 Troubleshooting Common Installation and Runtime Errors: Resolving Issues Effectively

Encountering errors is a normal part of software development.[6] Here are some common issues and their solutions:

- **"ModuleNotFoundError: No module named 'qiskit' or 'cirq'":**
  - **Solution:** Ensure that you've installed Qiskit or Cirq correctly using pip.[7]
  - Verify that you're running the Python interpreter within the

virtual environment where you installed the packages.

- Check your Python PATH environment variable.

- **"ImportError: DLL load failed" (Windows):**
  - **Solution:** This often indicates missing dependencies.
  - Install Microsoft Visual C++ Build Tools.
  - Ensure that your Python installation is compatible with the installed packages.

- **"PermissionError" (Linux/macOS):**
  - **Solution:** This usually occurs when pip doesn't have write access to the installation directory.
  - Try installing with sudo pip install <package>.
  - Consider using a virtual environment to avoid permission issues.

- **"Qiskit Aer not installed" or "Backend not found":**
  - ○ **Solution:** Install Qiskit Aer using pip install qiskit-aer.
  - ○ Ensure that you're using a compatible version of Qiskit and Aer.
- **"IBMProviderError: Account not available":**
  - ○ **Solution:** Ensure that you have an IBM Quantum Experience account and have configured your API token correctly.
  - ○ Use IBMQ.save_account(<your_api _token>) to save your account credentials.
- **Cirq simulation errors:**
  - ○ Ensure that your circuit is properly defined.
  - ○ Check for issues with the qubit definitions.
  - ○ Verify that all used gates are correctly defined.

- **General Troubleshooting Tips:**
  - **Update pip:** Run python -m pip install --upgrade pip.
  - **Update Qiskit/Cirq:** Run pip install --upgrade qiskit or pip install --upgrade cirq.
  - **Reinstall:** If all else fails, try uninstalling and reinstalling the packages.
  - **Search Online:** Search for the specific error message online. Many common errors have solutions posted on forums and Stack Overflow.
  - **Check Framework Documentation:** The Qiskit and Cirq documentation provide troubleshooting guides and FAQs.

B.3 List of Important Qiskit and Cirq Resources: Expanding Your Knowledge

Here's a list of essential resources to deepen your understanding and stay up-to-date:

- **Qiskit Documentation:**
  - qiskit.org/documentation
  - Provides comprehensive documentation, tutorials, and API references.
- **Cirq Documentation:**
  - quantumai.google/cirq/
  - Offers detailed documentation, examples, and tutorials.
- **Qiskit Textbook:**
  - qiskit.org/textbook
  - A free online textbook covering quantum computing fundamentals and Qiskit usage.
- **Cirq Tutorials:**
  - quantumai.google/cirq/tutorials
  - Provides a set of cirq tutorials.

- **IBM Quantum Experience:**
  - quantum-computing.ibm.com
  - Provides access to IBM's quantum computers and Qiskit Runtime.
- **Google Quantum AI Blog:**
  - quantumai.google/blog
  - Provides updates on Google's quantum computing research and Cirq developments.
- **Qiskit Slack Community:**
  - qiskit.slack.com
  - A community forum for Qiskit users.
- **Cirq GitHub Repository:**
  - github.com/quantumlib/Cirq
  - The official Cirq repository, where you can find source code and contribute to the project.
- **Stack Overflow (Quantum Computing Tag):**
  - stackoverflow.com/questions/tagged/quantum-computing

- A platform for asking and answering quantum computing questions.
- **Quantum Computing Report:**
  - quantumcomputingreport.com
  - Provides news, analysis, and resources on quantum computing.
- **arXiv (Quantum Physics):**
  - arxiv.org/archive/quant-ph
  - A repository of research papers on quantum physics and quantum computing.

By following these instructions and utilizing the provided resources, you'll be well on your way to mastering Qiskit and Cirq and exploring the fascinating world of quantum computing.

Appendix C: Glossary of Quantum Computing Terms

Quantum computing, with its unique concepts and terminology, can seem daunting at first. This glossary aims to demystify the field, providing clear and comprehensive definitions of key terms.

A

- **Adiabatic Quantum Computing (AQC):** A computational paradigm that solves problems by slowly evolving a quantum system from a known ground state to the ground state of a Hamiltonian encoding the problem's solution.
- **Amplitude Amplification:** A quantum technique, used in Grover's algorithm, to increase the probability of measuring the desired solution.[1]
- **Ansatz:** A parameterized quantum circuit used in variational quantum

algorithms to approximate the solution to a problem.[2]

B

- **Bloch Sphere:** A geometric representation of a single qubit's state, visualizing the superposition of $|0\rangle$ and $|1\rangle$.[3]
- **Bra-Ket Notation:** A standard notation in quantum mechanics for representing quantum states, using angle brackets ($\langle |$ and[4] $| \rangle$).

C

- **Classical Bit (Bit):** The fundamental unit of classical information, representing either 0 or 1.[5]
- **Coherence:** The ability of a quantum system to maintain superposition and entanglement.

- **Coherence Time:** The duration for which a quantum system maintains coherence before decoherence occurs.
- **Complex Number:** A number with both real and imaginary parts, essential for describing quantum amplitudes.[6]
- **Controlled Gate:** A quantum gate that applies an operation to a target qubit only if a control qubit is in a specific state.[7]
- **CNOT Gate (Controlled-NOT):** A fundamental two-qubit gate that flips the target qubit if the control qubit is $|1\rangle$.
- **Cryptography (Post-Quantum):** The field of developing cryptographic algorithms that are secure against attacks from both classical and quantum computers.[8]

D

- **Decoherence:** The loss of quantum coherence due to interactions with the environment.[9]
- **Density Matrix:** A mathematical representation of a quantum system's state, including mixed states (probabilistic mixtures of pure states).[10]
- **Digital Quantum Simulation:** Simulating a quantum system using a sequence of quantum gates on a quantum computer.

E

- **Eigenvalue/Eigenvector:** A scalar and a vector, respectively, that satisfy the equation $Av = \lambda v$, where A is a matrix.[11]
- **Entanglement:** A quantum phenomenon where two or more qubits become correlated, such that their states are interdependent.[12]

- **Error Correction (Quantum):** Techniques for protecting quantum information from errors caused by noise and decoherence.[13]

F

- **Fault Tolerance:** The ability of a quantum computer to perform computations reliably despite errors.
- **Feature Map (Quantum):** A mapping from classical data to a high-dimensional quantum Hilbert space, used in quantum machine learning.

G

- **Gate (Quantum):** A unitary operation that manipulates qubits, forming the building blocks of quantum circuits.[14]

- **Grover's Algorithm:** A quantum algorithm that provides a quadratic speedup for searching an unsorted database.[15]

H

- **Hadamard Gate (H Gate):** A single-qubit gate that creates a superposition of $|0\rangle$ and $|1\rangle$.
- **Hamiltonian:** An operator that describes the total energy of a quantum system.[16]
- **Hermitian Matrix:** A square matrix that is equal to its conjugate transpose, representing observables in quantum mechanics.[17]
- **Hilbert Space:** A complex vector space that describes all possible states of a quantum system.
- **Hybrid Quantum-Classical Algorithm:** An algorithm that combines classical and quantum computations to solve a problem.[18]

I

- **Interference (Quantum):** The phenomenon where quantum waves can constructively or destructively interfere, affecting probability amplitudes.[19]

K

- **Kernel (Quantum):** A function that measures the similarity between quantum states, used in quantum machine learning.
- **Key Distribution (Quantum - QKD):** A cryptographic protocol that uses quantum mechanics to establish a secure shared key between two parties.

L

- **Logical Qubit:** A qubit encoded using multiple physical qubits to protect it from errors.[20]

M

- **Measurement (Quantum):** The process of obtaining classical information from a quantum state, causing the state to collapse.[21]
- **Mixed State:** A statistical ensemble of pure quantum states, described by a density matrix.
- **Moment:** A time slice in a Cirq quantum circuit that contains a set of operations that are executed simultaneously.[22]

N

- **NISQ (Noisy Intermediate-Scale Quantum):** The current era of quantum computing, characterized by noisy and limited-qubit devices.[23]

- **No-Cloning Theorem:** A fundamental theorem stating that it is impossible to create an identical copy of an arbitrary unknown quantum state.[24]
- **Noise Model:** A mathematical description of the noise affecting a quantum system.

O

- **Observable:** A physical quantity that can be measured in a quantum system, represented by a Hermitian operator.[25]
- **Oracle:** A black box function used in quantum algorithms to mark solutions.
- **Operation:** In Cirq, an action performed on qubits, such as a gate or measurement.

P

- **Parameterized Quantum Circuit:** A quantum circuit with adjustable parameters, used in variational quantum algorithms.[26]
- **Pauli Gates (X, Y, Z):** Fundamental single-qubit gates that perform rotations around the x, y, and z axes of the Bloch sphere.[27]
- **Phase Kickback:** A technique used in quantum algorithms to transfer the phase information of a target qubit to a control qubit.[28]
- **Photon:** A particle of light used in quantum communication and some quantum computing implementations.[29]
- **Probability Amplitude:** A complex number associated with a quantum state, whose squared magnitude gives the probability of measuring that state.[30]

- **Pulse-Level Programming:** Control of quantum hardware at the level of individual pulses, allowing fine-grained manipulation of qubits.
- **Pure State:** A quantum state that can be described by a single state vector.

Q

- **QAOA (Quantum Approximate Optimization Algorithm):** A hybrid quantum-classical algorithm for solving combinatorial optimization problems.[31]
- **QASM (Quantum Assembly Language):** A textual representation of quantum circuits.
- **Qubit (Quantum Bit):** The fundamental unit of quantum information, capable of existing in a superposition of states.[32]
- **Quantum Annealing:** A quantum optimization technique that uses

quantum fluctuations to find the minimum energy state of a system.

- **Quantum Circuit:** A sequence of quantum gates and measurements that implement a quantum algorithm.[33]

- **Quantum Computer:** A device that uses quantum mechanics to perform computations.[34]

- **Quantum Control:** The ability to manipulate and control quantum systems with high precision.

- **Quantum Error Correction:** Techniques to protect quantum information from noise.[35]

- **Quantum Fourier Transform (QFT):** A quantum algorithm that efficiently computes the discrete Fourier transform.

- **Quantum Machine Learning (QML):** The application of quantum computing to enhance machine learning algorithms.[36]

- **Quantum Simulation:** Using a quantum computer to model and simulate quantum systems.
- **Quantum Teleportation:** A protocol for transferring an unknown quantum state from one location to another.[37]

S

- **Shor's Algorithm:** A quantum algorithm that efficiently factors large numbers, posing a threat to classical public-key cryptography.
- **Superdense Coding:** A quantum communication protocol that allows two classical bits to be transmitted using one qubit.
- **Superposition:** A quantum phenomenon where a qubit can exist in multiple states simultaneously.[38]
- **Surface Code:** A topological quantum error correction code that is

promising for building large-scale quantum computers.[39]

- **Syndrome Measurement:** A measurement used in quantum error correction to identify errors without collapsing the logical qubit state.[40]

T

- **Tensor Product:** A mathematical operation used to combine quantum states and operators.
- **Toffoli Gate (CCNOT Gate):** A three-qubit gate that flips the target qubit if both control qubits are $|1\rangle$.
- **Trotterization:** A technique for approximating the time evolution of a quantum system by breaking it into small steps.

U

- **Unitary Matrix:** A complex square matrix whose conjugate transpose is equal to its inverse, representing quantum gates.[41]

V

- **Variational Quantum Algorithm (VQA):** A hybrid quantum-classical algorithm that uses a parameterized quantum circuit to approximate the solution to a problem.
- **VQE (Variational Quantum Eigensolver):** A variational quantum algorithm used to find the ground state energy of a quantum system.
- **Virtual Environment:** An isolated Python environment that allows you to manage dependencies for specific projects.[42]

This glossary provides a foundation for understanding the language of quantum computing. As you delve deeper into the field, you'll encounter more specialized terms, but this comprehensive list will serve as a valuable reference.

Appendix D: Code Examples and Resources.

This appendix provides you with a wealth of practical resources to enhance your quantum computing journey. From readily accessible code examples to curated online resources, this section is designed to facilitate hands-on learning and exploration.

D.1 Links to GitHub Repository Containing All Code:

- **Repository   Name:** QuantumComputingExplorations
- **Link:** [Insert your GitHub repository link here – **Important:** You must create a GitHub repository and

populate it with the code examples from this book/notes.]

- **Description:** This repository contains all code examples presented throughout the book/notes, organized by chapter and topic. It serves as a practical resource for readers to experiment with quantum algorithms, simulations, and applications. The repository includes:
  - Qiskit code examples demonstrating quantum circuit construction, simulation, and hardware execution.
  - Cirq code examples showcasing advanced circuit design, noise modeling, and parameterized circuits.
  - Hybrid quantum-classical algorithm implementations, such as VQE and QAOA.
  - Quantum machine learning examples, including QSVMs and QNNs.

- Code examples demonstrating interoperability between Qiskit and Cirq.
- Instructions on how to run the code in various environments (local simulators, cloud platforms).

D.2 Links to Online Resources:

- **Qiskit Documentation:**
  - qiskit.org/documentation
  - The official Qiskit documentation, providing comprehensive tutorials, API references, and user guides.
- **Cirq Documentation:**
  - quantumai.google/cirq
  - The official Cirq documentation, offering in-depth tutorials, examples, and API references.
- **Qiskit Textbook:**

- qiskit.org/textbook
  - A free, interactive online textbook covering quantum computing fundamentals and Qiskit programming.
- **IBM Quantum Experience:**
  - quantum-computing.ibm.com
  - Provides access to IBM's quantum computers and Qiskit Runtime.
- **Google Quantum AI Blog:**
  - quantumai.google/blog
  - Offers insights into Google's quantum computing research and Cirq developments.
- **Amazon Braket:**
  - aws.amazon.com/braket
  - Provides access to quantum hardware from various providers.
- **Microsoft Azure Quantum:**
  - azure.microsoft.com/en-us/services/quantum

- Provides access to quantum hardware and services.
- **Quantum Computing Report:**
  - quantumcomputingreport.com
  - A comprehensive resource for quantum computing news, analysis, and research.
- **arXiv (Quantum Physics):**
  - arxiv.org/archive/quant-ph
  - A repository of pre-print research papers on quantum physics and quantum computing.
- **Quantum Information and Computation (QIC) Journal:**
  - Search for the journal online.
  - A leading academic journal in the field of quantum information.
- **Quantum Slack Channels:**
  - Search for Qiskit and other quantum computing slack channels.

○ Great for asking questions and getting help.

Appendix E: Further Reading and Research Papers – Diving Deeper into Quantum Knowledge

To further expand your knowledge and delve into cutting-edge research, here's a curated list of books and academic papers:

E.1 Books:

- **"Quantum Computation and Quantum Information" by Michael A. Nielsen and Isaac L. Chuang:** The definitive textbook on quantum computing.
- **"Programming Quantum Computers" by Eric R. Johnston, Nic Harrigan, and Mercedes Gimeno-Segovia:** A practical guide to quantum programming.

- **"Quantum Computing for Computer Scientists" by Noson S. Yanofsky and Mirco A. Mannucci:** A comprehensive introduction for computer scientists.
- **"Dancing with Qubits" by Robert Sutor:** An accessible introduction to quantum computing.
- **"Quantum Computing: From Linear Algebra to Physical Realizations" by Mikio Nakahara and Tetsuo Ohmi:** A more mathematically rigorous approach.
- **"An Introduction to Quantum Computing" by Phillip Kaye, Raymond Laflamme, and Michele Mosca:** A solid introduction.

E.2 Academic Papers:

- **"Shor's Algorithm: Polynomial-Time Algorithms for Prime Factorization and Discrete**

Logarithms on a Quantum Computer" by Peter W. Shor: The seminal paper on Shor's algorithm.

- "A Fast Quantum Mechanical Algorithm for Database Search" by Lov K. Grover: The foundational paper on Grover's algorithm.
- "Quantum Error Correction" by Peter W. Shor: The original paper on quantum error correction codes.
- "Fault-Tolerant Quantum Computation" by Daniel Gottesman: A key paper on fault-tolerant quantum computing.
- "The Variational Quantum Eigensolver Algorithm" by Alberto Peruzzo et al.: The original paper that introduced the VQE algorithm.
- "A Quantum Approximate Optimization Algorithm" by Edward Farhi et al.: The paper introducing the QAOA algorithm.

- Search for papers on arXiv, and in journals like Physical Review Letters, Nature Physics, and Quantum.

Index

By providing these resources, readers will continue their quantum computing education and contribute to the advancement of this exciting field.